Once You Go Black

D0776013

JUL 25 2007

SEXUAL CULTURES: New Directions from the Center for Lesbian and Gay Studies
General Editors: José Esteban Muñoz and Ann Pellegrini

Robert Reid-Pharr

Once You Go Black

Choice, Desire, and the Black American Intellectual

NEW YORK UNIVERSITY PRESS   New York and London

NEW YORK UNIVERSITY PRESS
New York and London
www.nyupress.org

Library of Congress Cataloging-in-Publication Data
Reid-Pharr, Robert, 1965–
Once you go Black : choice, desire, and the Black American intellectual /
Robert Reid-Pharr.
p.   cm. — (Sexual cultures)
Includes bibliographical references (p.   ) and index.
ISBN-13: 978-0-8147-7583-7 (acid-free paper)
ISBN-10: 0-8147-7583-7 (acid-free paper)
ISBN-13: 978-0-8147-7584-4 (pbk. : acid-free paper)
ISBN-10: 0-8147-7584-5 (pbk. : acid-free paper)
1. African Americans—Intellectual life—20th century. 2. African
American intellectuals—Biography. 3. African Americans—Race identity.
4. Masculinity—United States—History—20th century. 5. Racism—
United States—History—20th century. 6. African Americans—Sexual
behavior—History—20th century. 7. American literature—African
American authors—History and criticism. 8. Racism in literature.
9. Sex role in literature. 10. Sex in literature.   I. Title.
E185.86.R418 2007
305.896'07300904—dc22   2007000138

New York University Press books are printed on acid-free paper,
and their binding materials are chosen for strength and durability.

Manufactured in the United States of America
c 10 9 8 7 6 5 4 3 2 1
p 10 9 8 7 6 5 4 3 2 1

Contents

Acknowledgments

I am frankly amazed and a little embarrassed by the sheer amount of patience, generosity, and good will that have been shown to me and to *Once You Go Black* as we have developed over the last several years. The Alexander von Humboldt Foundation awarded me a research grant for the 2002–2003 academic year that enabled me to complete a large amount of work while also forming what I hope will be lifelong relationships with friends and colleagues in Berlin and elsewhere in Germany. Guenter Lenz of the Humboldt University of Berlin sponsored my application to the Humboldt Foundation and proved to be a wonderful host and mentor. Thomas Ebel ensured the survival of all the best parts of me, even during the most unforgiving Berlin winter and the fantastic spring and summer that followed. At home, my students and colleagues at the Graduate Center of the City University of New York daily surprise me with their intelligence, flexibility, skill, commitment, courage, and again that unsettling generosity. Our last executive officer, Joan Richardson, greatly facilitated my leave, while our current leader, Steve Kruger, has proven to be not only a fine administrator but also a selflessly giving intellectual. Three individuals, Fabio Parasecoli, Arnaldo Cruz-Malavé, and Wayne Koestenbaum, read complete drafts of this book. I thank them for their time and care, and I apologize for those rough patches in this work that I am certain would have been smoothed over if I had indeed taken all their advice to heart and mind. Earlier versions of chapters four and five appeared in the on-line journal *Cultural Matters*, issue I (fall 2001), and in Elahe Haschemi Yekani and Beatrice Michaelis's collection *Quer Durch die Geisteswissenschaften: Perspektiven der Queer Theory* (Quer Verlag, 2005). I read excerpts from *Once You Go Black* at George Mason University, the University of Washington, the University of Tennessee, Harvard University, Wesleyan University, Dartmouth College, the Humboldt University of Berlin, the Free

University of Berlin, Clark University, the Miami University of Ohio, the University of Michigan, and New York University. I would like to thank all of the individuals responsible for inviting me. In particular, I have to mention Heather Love, Henry Abelove, Donald Pease and Robyn Weigman, Stephanie Dunning, Winston Napier, Scott Trafton, Paul Smith, Samuel Delany, Phillip Brian Harper, and Shelly Eversley for the amazing conversations about my work that they helped to initiate.

Introduction

The Existential Negro

I refuse to speak from the point of view of the victim. The victim can have no point of view for precisely so long as he thinks of himself as a victim. The testimony of the victim as victim corroborates, simply, the reality of the chains that bind him—confirms and, as it were, consoles the jailer.

—James Baldwin, *The Evidence of Things Not Seen*

Being a Negro American involves a willed (who wills to be a Negro? I do!) affirmation of self as against all outside pressures—an identification with the group as extended through the individual self which rejects all possibilities of escape that do not involve a basic resuscitation of the original American ideals of social and political justice. And those white Negroes (and I do not mean Norman Mailer's dream creatures) are Negroes too—if they wish to be.

—Ralph Ellison, *Shadow and Act*

The book does not serve my freedom; it requires it. Indeed, one cannot address himself to freedom as such by means of constraint, fascination, or entreaties. There is only one way of attaining it; first, by recognizing it, then, having confidence in it, and finally requiring of it an act, an act in its own name, that is, in the name of the confidence that one brings to it.

—Jean-Paul Sartre, *Literature and Existentialism*

I invite you to imagine a rather comically American scenario. The intellectual, a promising young man of color, has made his way to one of the great capitals of Europe. He has established himself in a borrowed apartment, learned the rudiments of the native language, surrounded himself with books and music, all American of course, and settled down to write. But he is, as is often the case with Americans caught in that peculiar vertigo caused by travel, distracted. The news from home is not good. The rank stench of war reaches him from every corner. Troops mass on enemy borders; bombs explode on buses, killing housewives and office workers; missiles are fired into camps, dismembering refugees who look disturbingly similar to our intrepid intellectual. A great gray cloud of terrorism answered by terror hangs over his country, over countries he has never seen, and even over the airy, bright apartment that he has borrowed here in the center of this still war-scarred European capital.

He had planned to write during his year abroad (indeed the first he has ever had) a study of Black American intellectuals who came of age after the last of the great wars. He had thought to pay homage to that generation of male artists and critics to whom he feels most indebted, those who had grappled most assiduously with matters of race, gender, and sexuality, those who had been celebrated in his childhood as fine examples of genius, Black, American, genius. He finds himself stifled, however, distracted as he has said, because the work of celebration, of historical recovery, has become suddenly, if not inexplicably, a rather more complicated matter. The gift, the challenge that was given from that earlier generation to his own, was not, he believes, simply an impressive body of literature nor even the heroic and largely successful struggles to advance the civil and human rights of not only Black Americans but indeed much of the human community. It was not even that American people with crinkly hair and brown skin more or less similar to his own crinkly hair and brown skin have come, in some quarters, to be associated with the advance of liberal society. The even more profound gift, the warmly glowing coal that burns with a throbbing, impersonal heat when examined too closely is the knowledge that the Black American has not only had a great hand in the creation of America and thus the world but also and importantly that the Black American, quiet as it's kept, has had a substantial role in the creation of himself.

He believes that his community is not simply the inevitable result of slavery and segregation, the whip and the ugly snarl of the hound. Indeed he regularly reminds his compatriots of what he takes to be patently apparent. Even as we must memorialize and seek to undo the grave human tragedies enacted by our countrymen, and perhaps ourselves: the colonization of the African continent, the breathtaking waste of human life in the Middle Passage, the scourge of bondage that still warps the societies and cultures of Europe and the Americas, as well as the banal incivility and malice that were demonstrated during the long years of segregation, it is nonetheless true that the people most caught up in these ugliest of human dramas (the blacks, the Negroes, the coloreds) were never passive victims. Though Americans have not yet weaned themselves from a rhetoric in which people with almond-shaped eyes, sand-colored skin, strong Yankee accents, and addresses in Boston, Chicago, and New York have been ripped from their homelands, stripped of their cultures, and deposited, rather helplessly, in a world that they did not produce, a world in which they are, as it were, the last innocents, this does not change the fact that Black American people have accomplished a feat greater than the building of cities or empires. They have constructed one of the first truly modern communities, one with its roots just as securely in the resistance to slavery, colonization, conquest, and racial degradation as in these horrific realities themselves.

What would happen, the young man wonders, what worlds would collide, if students of American history and culture were to take seriously the idea that we all possess agency and indeed choice? He is stunned, in fact, that the existentialist maxim which so fascinated the generation of scholars who came before him, that experience precedes essence, seems never to be applied to the Black American community. Blackness is perhaps the most tradition-bound product that his country manufactures. And though his peers are all too eager to demonstrate the means by which black identity has been constructed, it seems that their arguments somehow always turn toward the metaphysical. That is to say, while one can see where the nuts and bolts of so-called racial distinction are situated within the basic structures of American culture, this does not mean that one might turn those nuts or adjust those bolts no matter how sophisticated our tools have become. Instead it seems that with one breath we admit that we live in a machine that has been constructed, while with the next we confess to having lost the basic knowledge of that machine's functioning.

Thus it is an article of faith with our young intellectual that the time has arrived for our advances in theoretical and historical analysis to come into sync with our rhetoric, our common sense. The Black American is not produced at the location at which the African was dehumanized, at the point at which he became a nigger. Niggers cannot clear forests, raise crops, build roads, fight wars, much less found universities or establish traditions of literature, art, and music. Instead, the Black American is produced at precisely that moment at which the attempt to dehumanize the African is met by the equally bold attempt to resist that dehumanization. That is to say, the Black American represents the moment of contradiction, the moment at which

3

the slaver must come to negotiate with the enslaved, the moment at which America itself comes into being.

Of course we are all aware of Hegel's provocative evocation of the confrontation between master and slave in which black identity is read as precisely the refusal of the master's anti-identitarian domination. The master strikes the slave, the slave strikes back, and thus a man is created. Our dirty little black and American secret, however, is that even though there are many moments in our history in which we have struck back, taken up arms, killed and been killed, there are many more in which we have cajoled, bargained, shuffled, run, used our cunning and our intellect to effect if not positive then hopefully less than deadly ends. Indeed one might quite easily make the provocative claim that the Black American has utilized sex and sexuality as a means by which to ensure the survival of black individuals and communities to a *much* greater extent than he has utilized violent confrontation, thus the evidence provided by all those almond-shaped eyes and all that sand-colored skin.

Our promising young man of color must wonder, however, at the ways in which this particular narrative of identity formation seems always to be subjected to the most basic, indeed the most exhausted, of readings. As with Frederick Douglass's fateful struggle with the slave breaker, Covey, it seems that we can only understand the articulation of black freedom as a singular event. The great fists of a godly Douglass smote the wicked Covey, and at that moment a race was born. This action is never repeated, nor does it ever change, as the identity that was given voice on that fateful day in eastern Maryland was a finished and indeed sacred product. Douglass chose, and no other choosing has been allowed. Moreover, other forms of choice, other means by which one might articulate distinction, are scarcely perceptible to current generations of Americans.[1]

Strangely, it seems that Americans articulate race in much the same manner that René Girard suggests that western novelists articulate rivalry and desire. Indeed the young intellectual is shocked to find himself wondering if race is not actually lived *as* desire. (Racial) combatants are absolutely certain that they are distinct from their rivals. Nonetheless their behaviors, their needs, their wants, their grimy obsessions are remarkably similar to those of the so-called enemy. On either side the dominant gesture is one of negation. "I am not that vile thing which I hate." But strangely this gesture always reestablishes the intimacy of the rivals' relationship. Moreover, this habitual and ritualized articulation of distinction alerts the outsider to the fact that it is not so much history that structures rivalry as a simple discursive structure whose only purpose is to encourage the constant repetition of a pathetic "no."[2]

But as anyone skilled in the interpretation of puns and jokes knows, there are always at least two levels on which even the most basic statements might be read. One must always distinguish what the lips say from what the eyes speak. Indeed, as Girard suggests, the violence, the horror, the panic that underwrites the clumsy idea that one is altogether distinct from the horrifying other is itself evidence of a desire for and identification with the other that is so very profound that it must be constantly denied if "traditional" distinctions are to be maintained.

It is of course not the intention of the author to offer a treatment of, say, the southern plantation that describes it yet again as a sort of sadistic, interracial bordello. Not quite. He understands quite clearly that much of the actual conflict between masters and servants in the United States has been over simple questions of labor. How much? How difficult? When? That said, he would remind his reader that his concern in these pages is not so much with the physical products produced by Americans as with those most artificial of products, the various identity schemes grouped under rubrics of race, sexuality, gender, and class. Moreover, caught in the updraft produced by queer theory, it seems patently apparent to him that the struggle we imagine and constantly reiterate between master and slave is not only sexualized but homoerotic and performative as well. Thus we should attempt to understand the ways in which the interracial tableau on display in the master/slave dyad reiterates not so much American phobias about the intermingling (sexual and otherwise) of "the races" as our own rather strict ideas about how these "phobias" ought rightly to be performed. I would suggest, in fact, that the constancy of the rhetoric of master/slave struggle, the ways in which it has become ritualized in contemporary society, works precisely to stave off a too close examination of the fact that this struggle has as much to do with the will to maintain obviously artificial distinctions between communities and persons as with any righteous desire for "racial" justice. We are not simply concerned with who gets access to what resources but also with how one might distinguish oneself from one's neighbor. Thus each racial iteration is, in fact, a performative act, not terribly different from that of the child who dresses himself in sheets and announces the arrival of a ghost.

The difficulty for the American intellectual then is not the complexity or the opaque nature of this idea but instead its obviousness. "Race" is so very thin an idea, one dependent at best upon an embarrassingly clumsy jumble of notions about origin and genealogy, all of which are in turn dependent upon the naive belief that current sexual norms are not only ancient but patently natural. That is to say, as sexuality is determined by nature then so must be race. The queer subject in this scenario is not simply that person who does not participate in these performances. Nor is it that subject who points to race and says vehemently "performance" and "ritual." Instead the queer subject is that figure who not only acknowledges that we perform racial difference but also that we perform our ignorance of this performance, that though "race" comes freighted with all the weight of history, it is nonetheless farcical and obviously so. But to suggest this simple fact, to note the reality that we know very well how shallow our conceptions of difference are, is slightly akin to pulling off one's mask during carnival, an act that is both somewhat rude *and* queer.

Hopefully it is clear by now that part of what inspires *Once You Go Black* is a desire to draw together the insights of Black American cultural and literary criticism with those of queer theory. In particular, one might take *Once You Go Black* as a challenge for black queers (the term seems oddly redundant) to pick up the gauntlet thrown down by Slavoj Žižek, who reminds us that it is not true that simply because a subject occupies a position that is "marginal" or has an understanding of the world that is "partial" that he cannot know and express truth. On the contrary, Žižek suggests that "partiality" is the only human condition that is, in fact, universal. Indeed as each of us inhabits our own specificity it may also be the case that the subject who embraces the fact of his specificity has the best chance to recognize the reality of the universal embedded within the specific.[3]

Thus the author refuses the assumption that alone in his apartment, slightly off balance as he attempts to make sense of the reality of his country far from Carolina beaches or New York highways, that he is either victim or hopelessly exceptional. Instead he takes his "exceptionality" to be that which binds him to the rest of humanity. Or in a less grandiose posture he would suggest that the "queer space" that he inhabits is itself emblematic of the spaces that all intellectuals, black, American, and otherwise, have, in fact, chosen. The room, the key, those guineas—these are essential to anyone who would take up the mantle of the intellectual, particularly the engaged intellectual. Moreover, in his willful misreading of the term "queer," our earnest young man of color means first and foremost to privilege the radically antitraditionalist aesthetic that fuels this study. Indeed he suggests that the game for the contemporary intellectual is always played in the present. Our gallant efforts to narrate our various peoples' separation one from the other always devolve (our continual references to an ancient past notwithstanding) into the clumsy insults and platitudes that one sees most often between erotic rivals. "I am different from you but nonetheless I want what you've got."

These are the very questions scattered haphazardly on the desk in the bright apartment as the promising young man of color attempts to line up his own sense of truth with the political and social realities that daily beset him. He believes that it is his role to confront his readers with the reality of their freedom, with the reality that they do, in fact, have the ability to choose, to move if you will, even if not within conditions of their own making. He argues then for a much more expansive conception of freedom of choice. One might not only choose one's rooms, one's books, one's music, and one's sexual partners, but also and importantly one might choose one's identity, indeed one's race.

This is not simply to reiterate the now well-worn argument that the forms of racial identity with which we are familiar are certainly not inevitable but, on the contrary, have been established by individuals, communities, and governments acting on historically and culturally specific circumstances. Nor is it the author's intention to insert poorly considered ideas about the necessity of a certain spontaneity or individuality in the production of identity. Instead he hopes first and foremost to challenge the sense of inevitability that he sees far too often in the work of many students of race and ethnicity. He plans to take seriously the idea that current generations of Americans are indeed agents and not simply products of history. Thus he would remind his readers that the twentieth century with its crumbling of empires, its massive migrations and displacements, its genocidal wars, and importantly its stunning advances in technology was not an epoch, as some would claim, in which we witnessed a deadening of our awareness of human diversity. Instead exactly the opposite might be true. The century saw an incredible proliferation of not only varieties of difference but also an amazing development of the technologies that allow for the reinforcement and policing of those differences. Indeed where our young intellectual may be most distinct from his peers is in his almost religious belief that standing behind this proliferation of differences have been free and self-conscious human subjects who have provided profound legacies of culture and politics to our own generation but who nonetheless cannot—and should not—have the final word on what we choose for our own futures.

Critics will argue, perhaps fairly, that this reiteration of choice as a necessary element in the production of identity and community as well as the creation of a new "raced" and "sexed" map of the choices that we make in America as Americans cannot be grounded in either the realities of history or the rigors of philosophy. One is of course returned to both the matter of the slave's presumed lack of choice and to the question of what makes "choice" a so-called human right at all. In considering these objections, we must contend with the fact that the belief that enslaved Africans and their ancestors were deprived of choice is a central element within the mythic structure that underwrites Black American identity. The history of the Black American, a history often made bitter by the avarice and stupidity of his compatriots, has been precisely the struggle to choose. If one can imagine a prototypical Black American subject, then it is surely he who struggles to choose his own work, home, family, his own destiny. Thus for those of us who would still take up the project of a progressive American Studies, a progressive Americanism, those who understand ourselves to walk in paths prepared by people who lacked choice, if not will, there seems no question but that the challenge that we face is the task of attempting as best we can to extract the radical potentialities embedded within the very practices of choice for which we—and our ancestors—have longed.

Certainly part of what the author intends is to transport the language of choice, a language that many might remark as queer, into the formal apparatuses supporting the articulation of Black American difference. He would also contend that there is no opting out of this process of choosing. Indeed his challenge to those who would suggest that the weight of history disallows any efficacious manipulation of the cultural and ideological apparatuses that underwrite so-called racial distinction is to suggest that their contention that they cannot or will not choose is, in fact, an affirmation of the racial status quo. Racial distinction continues to be so fixed an entity within American culture precisely because we like it that way. Moreover each shrug of the shoulders, every sigh of defeat, all the tiny methods by which we resign ourselves to a self-imposed powerlessness operates as stunning proof of our positive commitment to maintaining racial distinction—and indeed racism—as key elements in the ideological apparatuses that underwrite contemporary American culture.

It should be obvious at this juncture that the goals of this study are not only historical and theoretical but moral and ethical as well. The author hopes first and foremost to help reemphasize the necessity of one's taking personal moral responsibility for one's nation (or the choice that one has made in one's nation) and thereby one's world that Ralph Ellison, among many others, articulated so eloquently. He believes, in fact, that the "forced choice" with which the Black American must wrestle is a sort of inevitable (Black) American patriotism, a recognition that by necessity one must throw in one's lot with the oppressors, "the whites," because, in fact, these oppressors are not only one's compatriots but also in a sense one's ancestors and one's progeny. Ellison writes,

> the values of my own people are neither "white" nor "black," they are American. Nor can I see how they could be anything else, since we are a people who are involved in the texture of the American experience. And indeed, today the most dramatic fight for American ideals is being sparked by black Americans. Significantly, we are the only black peoples who are not fighting for separation from the "whites," but for a fuller participation in the society which we share with "whites." And it is of further significance that we pursue our goals precisely in terms of American Constitutionalism.[4]

Sitting in a bright apartment that he has borrowed here in the center of this still war-scarred European capital, somewhat stunned as rumors of war turn into preparations for war, the young intellectual cannot imagine an end to what he believes is madness unless the various communities to which he owes allegiance, and in particular the Black American and Gay and Lesbian communities, understand the need for their total moral investment in the future of the United States and take full responsibility for their nation, this wonderful, wicked child they have created. In keeping with these claims he will suggest that it is necessary that we begin the difficult work of historicizing what he has come to think of as racial desire. The question he asks is how did we end up in this strange situation in which we all agree upon the "fact" of the social construction of race while nonetheless never really accepting the idea that this construction might be dismantled. Indeed though we live within a society that we must continually reconstruct, we somehow imagine that even the most petty of our petty prejudices are, in fact, timeless, natural, outside the realm of the social. Race may be a clumsy, obnoxious, somewhat dangerous entity, but pity the fool who suggests that we just ask it to go play elsewhere.

Thus our young man of words turns to an ugly American joke told most often by his black compatriots as he searches for the title of his study. "Once you go black, you never go back." Is it true? he wonders. For if it is, if black identity and, in particular, black sexuality has the ability to reshape human subjectivity, then perhaps the answer for his nation is for all of its citizens to recognize the possibility—and indeed inevitability—of becoming black, of claiming one's proper place among the descendants of slaves, the architects of a great, if half finished, nation. If it is not true (and he suspects that it is not), then it becomes necessary that all Americans ask just how efficacious our racial distinctions actually are. We are a nation brimming with black pride, black consciousness, and black people, but this does not, it seems, make us less cruel or prone to blood-letting. These are among the most significant of the questions to which he has been led by the generation that precedes him. He has been to the mountaintop, as it were. It is a long way down to the other side.

I

In a brilliantly realized meditation on the status of racial ideology in contemporary American society, Thomas Holt reminds us that it is now commonplace for American intellectuals to stress the socially constructed nature of all manner of identity formations, particularly race. The problem that Holt rightly points to, however, is that though this constructivist mode is universally recognized as correct inside American universities, it is rather embarrassingly absent from the discussions of "race" that take place outside of academia, including those that significantly affect social policy. Holt suggests that the reason for this may be that the rhetoric of "social constructedness" has about it an "air of unreality that may limit its influence."[5] On the one hand, it is quite easy for contemporary American intellectuals to suggest that there is no such thing as race, while, on the other, we continue to refer to supposed "racial communities."

The problem becomes particularly difficult for those of us involved in the study of Black American history and culture because we risk either conceding to outmoded and regressive ways of thinking about human identity and diversity or devaluing as "unreal" or "immaterial" a history and culture that many of us take to be precious. Holt does suggest a way out of this dilemma. He reminds us that the very notion of social construction begs the question of historical change and continuity. In the American context this would mean that we must purge ourselves of the conceit that there is a universal, transhistorical "blackness," one that encompasses the realities of ancient Africa and our enslaved ancestors in the Americas as well as current generations of Afro-Americans, Afro-Cubans, Afro-Brazilians, Afro-Britains, Afro-Germans, and any persons or communities with even the vaguest of connections to the so-called mother continent. Put another way, one might say that while it may be the case that one drop of black blood makes one black, this is true only to the extent that the validity of U.S. conceptions of "racial" identity are acceded to both inside and outside the fifty states. Again the point here is to demonstrate the ways in which American intellectuals have produced a fetish of what they take to be the profundity, the depth of our most cherished—if not our most hallowed—historical narratives. Though much of our work in cultural studies has turned on the articulation of more and more complicated identity narratives, it is simply not the case that these particular iterations are the only narratives that are possible.

Holt works then to offer a much more rigorously historicized account of what "race" does and does not signify in the contemporary American context, stressing that we have only recently moved beyond an era in which Fordist economic and industrial organization dominated the social structures of the so-called developed world. From the moment of Henry Ford's introduction of modern assembly methods in his Detroit auto plants during the early part of the twentieth century to the oil crisis and deep recession in the United States during the 1970s, the economic and social life of what we euphemistically term "the West" was dominated by an emphasis on the mass production of goods for what was once imagined to be an endlessly expanding consumer market, much of it made up of the very workers responsible for turning raw materials into mass-produced items.

The U.S. government itself led the drive to reorient the American economy away from its reliance on small-scale farming and production, achieving its greatest successes during the 1930s with the enactment of Franklin Roosevelt's New Deal, a far-reaching set of legislative responses to the severe industrial and economic crises that had been brought about by the stock-market crash of 1929 and the subsequent depression. The Social Security and National Labor Relations Acts of 1935, the National Industrial Recovery Act of 1933, not to mention such agencies as the Works Project Administration, the National Youth Administration, and later the Fair Employment Practices Commission, were designed to abate stress and conflict in American society by bringing government into a heretofore unheard of role as mediator between labor and capital. Perhaps more significantly for the Black American population, the industrial codes enacted by Roosevelt's administration ensured industrial workers of minimum wages, a legal limit to the amount of time one could be required to work, and most importantly the right to organize. At the same time, the New Deal largely ignored the interests of nonindustrial workers, including some 37 percent of Black American workers employed as agricultural laborers and another 29 percent employed as domestics. This rather shocking "oversight" was exacerbated by the almost total collapse of the cotton industry and a series of government policies that favored the interests of large, mechanized farming concerns over those of small landowners.[6]

The end result was that the heavy flow of Black Americans who had migrated from rural areas to cities in the South, Midwest, Far West, and especially the Northeast became a veritable flood. Answering the sharp need for labor in the industrialized sections of the country brought about by the outbreak of World War I—and the subsequent end to European immigration— at least 500,000 Black Americans migrated from the rural South between 1917 and 1920 alone, while 750,000 made their way north and west between 1920 and 1930. This was followed by a breathtaking 1,599,000 migrants between the years of 1940 and 1950. Thus a community that was once almost exclusively associated with the country had turned to the city, had laid down the hoe and picked up, or rather attempted to pick up, the hammer.[7]

I have written elsewhere that one of the most common mistakes made by American historians is the too heavy emphasis on the fact that Black American culture has deep roots in slavery and more generally the life of the rural South. In relation to the question of the foundations of Black American literature in early national and antebellum America I have argued that though one regularly hears of the tradition of Black American writing leaping fully formed from the rice paddies of Louisiana or the tobacco fields of Virginia, the clear truth is that almost all Black American writers who published texts before Emancipation lived and worked in the urban North. Moreover, I have suggested that this was not simply a matter of the nominal freedom that these individuals enjoyed after the close of slavery in that region but also an effect of the particular stresses caused by the simple fact of urbanization. The first large Black American communities in the Northeast, those of Philadelphia, Boston, Rochester, New Haven, and especially New York, were themselves composed largely of migrants, persons who during the antebellum period either made their way from villages in the Northeast or escaped from slavery in the South to seek a better life for themselves in these quickly developing black enclaves. Thus what one finds in the earliest Black American novels, to take but one example, is an abiding interest in how it is that one might describe the rather incredible changes that these authors were witnessing—that is to say, how to describe the formation of a community.[8] I would suggest then that scholars of Black American history and culture are wrong when they assume the inevitability of a specifically black tradition of writing. And even more to the point, I am both perplexed and concerned by the unquestioned assumption that as we possess a long-established (writing) culture, there is no room for the Black American intellectual to reimagine the basic modes of black culture.

In stressing this point, I hope to clarify why I believe it is absolutely necessary that contemporary critics develop even more sophisticated and expansive theoretical tools to explore Black American intellectual and cultural life of the twentieth century, particularly literature. It is not enough simply to remark the fact that black writers of say the Harlem Renaissance were responding in their writing to a new set of conditions, the new urbanization that indeed would become the hallmark of Black American culture. This is though I am fully aware that themes of migration, urban poverty and discrimination, alienation and flight, to name just the most common, are abundant in twentieth-century black writing. Still, we risk short-circuiting our work if we stop with the simple question of the city—as the city has, in a sense, always existed in Black American literature. Or perhaps the real truth of the matter is that Black American literature has always existed in the city. The more significant question, however, is what difference do the changes that took place in American urban spaces between the 1850s and the 1950s (as well as the meanings attached to those changes) make not only in the production of Black American literature but also in Black American identity itself. If we are to maintain the rigorous historicism that is necessary for us to move beyond the trap of an empty rhetoric of social construction, then we will have to admit that the "blackness" described by the fugitive slave and the "blackness" proudly articulated by the radical memoirist of the 1960s are, in fact, two different things, even though both authors might have haunted the same Philadelphia streets.

Certainly the most obvious and perhaps most reasonable critique of this line of thought would be to stress the fact that both these moments of Black American migration, or more precisely (Black) American community deformation and reformation, were put in motion by the will of the state to control more efficiently the labor of slaves, ex-slaves, and their descendants. Indeed one might quite rationally claim that the construction of black enclaves outside of the rural South allowed for the higher visibility of the Black American population. Thus the "black" who in the rural South could not be distinguished from his "white" compatriots with a casual glance or a quick tug at stubbornly knotted hair could perhaps have his "race" recognized if he had the proper address, such that today the name "125th Street" still signifies "black" no matter how many blond ringlets might be seen bouncing down Harlem avenues.

Further, once one understands that the practice of segregation was, by definition, a largely urban affair (streetcars, buses, theaters, parks, libraries, swimming pools, and of course schools and universities) then it becomes easier to understand how the production of the urban ghetto allowed for the maintenance of a community of workers who might service (white) civil society while never being allowed to participate fully within it. From New York to Dakar, Chicago to Johannesburg, one of the great innovations of global capital has been the ability of white-supremacist states to "allow" so-called black service workers into "white" areas long enough to do the cleaning and the mending, the feeding of the "workers" and the tidy closing up of shop, then shuttling them rather efficiently back to "traditional black areas," where they might be carefully restricted from utilizing the very services and resources that they themselves provided. And if one was confused as to what a black actually was, one had only to look out the window at 5 p.m. or so to see "blacks" dutifully arranging themselves for transport back to their "native" areas.

I should just go ahead and state straightforwardly here that part of the reason that I am so resistant to notions of a profound black tradition that not only underwrites but dictates contemporary black cultural production is that I recognize that these same ideas underwrite logics of segregation and apartheid. Indeed I might remind my readers that the Southern Agrarian critics associated with Vanderbilt University in Tennessee couched their rather self-serving racism within claims that the deep traditions of the agrarian and segregated South should not and could not be challenged. It is then precisely this tendency to treat tradition as sacred that I believe remains unchallenged in the current practice of (Black) American Studies.

Perhaps my arguments will be easier to digest if I point out that legal segregation in the United States is a phenomenon that does not, in fact, have its roots in slavery but instead in the response to black political and economic insurgency during and immediately after Reconstruction. The Supreme Court's painfully reactionary *Plessy v. Ferguson* decision of 1896 upheld a law enacted in Louisiana in 1890 mandating the segregation of the races in public transport. That is to say, thirty years after the close of slavery and nearly twenty years after the end of Reconstruction the court upheld a law that specifically sought to further disable already essentially disenfranchised free blacks, who, particularly in Louisiana, were eager to compete in the quickly developing commercial and industrial sectors of the American economy, as evidenced by the very streetcar from which an extremely fair Homer Plessy was ejected. Interestingly, Plessy himself did not accept the label "black." Much of his indignation turned on the fact that as he looked like a "white person" and held only a minority of "black blood," he should by rights be allowed to seat himself among his peers in the white car. And though we might find Plessy's arguments obscene, it is important that we understand that they were not illogical. Or to state the matter from another direction, our contemporary belief that Plessy was a brother should be understood as exactly what it is, ideology, and not the inevitable outcome of black tradition.

Here then is the rub. For in antebellum Louisiana, Louisiana of the 1850s, Homer Plessy would not so easily have been classed with his fellow compatriots "of African descent." Louisiana most notoriously, but other southern states and locales as well, did indeed recognize and act upon legal and social distinctions between "blacks" and other "persons of color." I would argue, therefore, that what was accomplished with the Plessy decision was the federalization of a newly evident rigor in the application of the "one-drop" rule. The court insisted on the very notion of a profound and presumably unchanging racial distinctiveness with which we are familiar today. Thus within the modern United States a new set of meanings was attached to the sexual performances of "black" and "white" citizens. The old social distinctions developed in and by slavery were no longer appropriate for the new circumstances of the quickly industrializing United States. It is in this way that Plessy had an uncomfortable and unfamiliar "black" identity thrust upon him by no less an entity than the Supreme Court in order not so much to further harass Black Americans as to liberate the state from antebellum conventions of race and in this way to allow it much greater dexterity in its efforts to mobilize and control an increasingly urban workforce.[9] I would suggest then that the enactment of a segregated public sphere was a brutal first stage in a process of not only the manipulation of black labor but also, in fact, the creation of black labor *as* black labor; or to put the matter more bluntly *Plessy v. Ferguson* was in an odd way a necessary antecedent to the New Deal. Moreover, in both instances the logic of Black American peculiarity was built on the idea of an ancient distinction between black and white, an idea that proved to be shockingly powerful even though it was so obviously belied by basic realities of how "race" had been lived in the nation's recent past.

I should say again that what I am after here is a more rigorous historicization of racial desire. Specifically, I want to suggest that what we take to be ancient rivalries between master and slave may, in fact, be nothing more or less than the carefully orchestrated efforts by American elites to rationalize thinking about race and identity for twentieth-century Americans. It is worth pointing out in this regard that the racial category "mulatto" was not dropped from the census until 1920. The ability of the state to clearly divine the difference between the black and the white was not accomplished until almost the eve of Roosevelt's ambitious efforts to bring the country out of the Depression. Perhaps more startling still is that in 1900, a scant four years after the *Plessy* decision, W. E. B. Du Bois made the now well-known, if often misinterpreted, statement, "the world problem of the twentieth century is the problem of the color line." I have argued, in another context, that this famous statement and the address before the American Negro Academy from which it is taken, "The Present Outlook for the Dark Races of Mankind," have been rather woefully underanalyzed.[10] The way in which the statement is most often discussed speaks to a continual simplification of Du Bois's thinking. Most commentators prefer of course the more compact version of the aphorism that Du Bois included in *The Souls of Black Folk*: "The problem of the twentieth century is the problem of the color line." When we drop "world" from the quotation, however, this allows us to continue a sloppy logic in which one imagines that for Du Bois the "Negro Problem," as articulated in the United States, was ultimately indistinguishable from the colonization of the many nations of Africa, Asia, the Caribbean, Central and South America. Moreover, it demonstrates a serious lack of appreciation for the radically progressive nature of Du Bois's stance as both political theorist and activist.

Du Bois, himself given during much of his life to celebrating his mixed-race heritage, was not simply announcing what ultimately was a quite obvious point: race and racialism pervade every aspect of modern society. Instead he was suggesting, in the context of the nationalist-leaning American Negro Academy, that not only would Black American activists and intellectuals have to act in concert with "colored" activists and intellectuals from around the globe, but perhaps more importantly that the old American distinction between black and mulatto, the very distinction refused by the Supreme Court in *Plessy v. Ferguson,* would have to be given up by the "black" community itself.[11]

I mean to suggest that Du Bois chooses the very modern forms of Black American identity (and desire) with which we are familiar today; he chooses to accept the contention that no matter the world of difference that may exist between the fairest of "mulattoes" and the darkest of "Negroes," no matter their specificity or partiality, it is nonetheless possible to imagine a "universal (colored) subject," as it were, precisely by paying attention to the specific identity formations housed under that awkward label "Dark Races of the World." Thus one might raise "black" identity to the level of the universal by paying strict attention, as Du Bois himself does, to the fact that blackness is never, as those nine members of the Court undoubtedly imagined, a final answer but always a site of contradiction, always, in a sense, a question. By doing so, one might resist the white-supremacist efforts of the American state by precisely *not* refusing the newly formed racial identity recently fashioned for "black" citizens but instead foregrounding the theoretical and social instability of that identity, an instability that by necessity must be met by the sheer weight of human resolve in order to resist the cynicism inherent in the state's racialist claims. "Who wills to be a Negro? I do!"

Again, I hope that my readers will not take my efforts to represent the fact that Black American identity is not only socially constructed but also historically contingent as but an attempt to revamp vaguely sophisticated and ultimately solipsistic social constructivist arguments. I would point out, however, that my primary concern in *Once You Go Black* is not to correct the historical record per se but instead to remind current generations of Americans that they are not only the products of history but its agents as well. When I suggest, therefore, that Black American identity has been chosen (both for and by us), I do mean to focus attention on the inevitable questions of ethics and social responsibility that are bound up with the idea of free choice. Further, I am unwilling to concede, at this juncture, that these questions are applicable only to the aggregate and not the individual. On the contrary, I cannot conceive of how a nation might choose between war or peace, stagnation or progress in the absence of the people who live within it. This is even when the nation's subjects are most severely abused and exploited.

My deployment of the rhetoric of freedom of choice is designed, therefore, specifically to remind us of discussions among feminists, "queers," and others that take the individual's ability to choose—or not to choose—family, intimacy, parenthood, and so forth as a basic human right. Continuing in this vein, one might suggest that this same individual has the right to choose—or again not to choose—ethnicity, community, and "race." All that proper selecting of mates has, in fact, exactly the effect of allowing one to preselect, if you will, one's race, or at least the race of one's children. And I do mean to gesture here toward the stunning ways in which the common sense of sexual and erotic choice has changed over the past several decades. What were once thought to be unassailable boundaries of desire have been demonstrated to be nothing other than shabby forms of propaganda. Hopefully then this understanding will help us to bring into greater focus the stakes surrounding American efforts to maintain and police racial distinction. What the Supreme Court itself understood was that Homer Plessy, with all the good looks and striking manners of a New Orleans Creole, might very easily have been chosen. He might also have chosen. He might have looked across the space of the streetcar into a pink or brown face and said, "yes that is the one." But if this had been allowed, if the "black" might indiscriminately choose the "white" (and in a sense this is the very drama that Hegel narrates), then suddenly those newly minted racial distinctions would have meant nothing. And more to the point, Americans might have begun to understand the ways in which eros and desire have been disciplined in this country and put to the service of industry, commerce, and the state.

You will indulge me as I continue to chisel away at this point. But in truth the notion of the Black American's lack of choice is so deeply embedded within the American common sense that one must remain constantly vigilant lest its more pernicious aspects slip into one's own writing and thinking. This notion, the blackness of blackness, reaches its highest levels of sophistication when self-styled progressive theorists and activists begin to see the Black American community as a sort of internal American colony. Thus the Black American is understood as not *American* at all but instead as a pre-sumably African captive, waiting for rescue or liberation, whichever comes first.[12] This was the very idea at the center of the Communist Party's adoption in 1928 of a so-called Black Belt thesis, a policy that worked specifically to treat the Negro struggle for civil rights in the United States as but one more emanation of the worldwide struggle against imperialism. The Party's declaration reads in part,

> [We] must come out openly and unreservedly for the right of Negroes to self-determination in the Southern states, where the Negroes form a majority of the population. . . . The Negro question in the United States must be treated in its relation to the Negro question and struggles in other parts of the world. The Negro race everywhere is an oppressed race. Whether it is a minority (U.S.A., etc.), majority (South Africa), or inhabits a so-called independent state (Liberia, etc.), the Negroes are oppressed by imperialism.[13]

I should rush to say that in many ways I am very much in agreement with the sentiments expressed here. I do believe that it is not only logical but imperative that the so-called Negro question in the United States be treated *in relation to* the "Negro question[s] and struggles in other parts of the world." I also want to distance myself from those American intellectuals who still see fit to celebrate our country's sorry and costly history of anti-Communism. Indeed to continue to represent oneself as anti-Communist in the context of the contemporary United States is not only to wallow in a misplaced nostalgia but also to remove oneself from the world of actually existing political and social struggle. More important still is the fact that, especially during the early part of the twentieth century, the Communist Party USA was easily one of the most significant civil-rights institutions in the United States and perhaps the only party that was truly democratic, in the sense of allowing and encouraging participation by black citizens, causing no less a political pragmatist than New York congressman Adam Clayton Powell to make the observation that "today there is no group in America, including the Christian Churches, that practices racial brotherhood one-tenth as much as the Communist Party."[14]

Still, this does not change the fact that there was a rather rushed departure of prominent black intellectuals from the Party (Richard Wright's being perhaps the most spectacular) that cannot be explained solely by the intensity of harassment by governments, private institutions, and individuals. Nor can it be fully explained in the manner suggested by Harold Cruse, among others, as a result of Communist arrogance in relation to Black Americans and in particular the CPUSA's sudden shift to an antiwar position after the signing of the Nazi-Soviet Pact in 1939, a shift made more maddening still by the Communist adoption of an equally prowar stance in 1941 when the Germans invaded the Soviet Union.[15] The end result was that even as the American Communist leadership demanded that members support a united front against the Nazis, their ability to lead had been substantially undermined by their own equivocation and by the fact that many Communists and fellow travelers began to chafe at the idea of a party whose attention was first and foremost on the problems of the Soviet Union and not those of the United States itself. Perhaps the greatest evidence of this divided loyalty was the fact that the American leadership discouraged the Black American–led "Double V for Victory" campaign against fascism abroad and racism at home, arguing that militant struggle against segregation in the armed forces and job discrimination in American industry would undermine the war effort.

Even so, it must be recognized that there was both a push and a pull of Black American intellectuals out of the Party. The pull might rightly be characterized by both the stark reality of anti-Communism that began to take hold fully in the United States during World War II as well as the serious missteps made by Communists in order to ensure the security of the Soviet Union. The question of the push, however, is a somewhat more complicated matter. It is indeed as much a factor of the theorization of the "Negro Question" within the Party as it is a question of the political practice of Communists and anti-Communists. I would suggest, in fact, that the Communists' Black Belt thesis was in many ways simply the opposite side of the coin of capitalist manipulations of black labor that were at the center of both the *Plessy v. Ferguson* decision and the New Deal. The Negro Community, in both instances, is not understood as a complicated entity made up of many individuals but instead as a sort of tendency within labor, a tendency with a never changing set of desires and rivalries, a tendency always counterpoised to global capital and the so-called white man. Thus for the Communist Party there is ultimately no distinction between the Black American and "Negroes in various parts of the world." They are all products of a transnational—and seemingly transhistorical—imperialism whose only real challenger is the Party itself. Within this logic, Communists were absolutely correct to ask

Black Americans to subsume their interests within those of the Soviet Union. As the Soviet Republics were the center of Communist insurgency and thus the only real hope for an end to imperialism, their protection was absolutely essential if the Black American, or any Negro for that matter, was ever to achieve his own freedom.

What I have been attempting to do is to establish some of the texture of the rather complicated terrain of politics and ethics that confronted Black American intellectuals during the middle years of the twentieth century. I have suggested that, understood only as a community of laborers, Black Americans were trapped between the rock of rank capitalist domination and the hard place of an equally self-interested and Communist-dominated anticapitalism. In both instances, moreover, the instruction given to Black American communities and activists was to wait, to allow themselves the time necessary to become fully modernized and thus fully articulate members of the social whole. This is, in fact, the crux of Booker T. Washington's appeal to the nation during the latter part of the nineteenth century and the early part of the twentieth. The image that he utilized in his 1895 Atlanta Cotton States Exposition speech of ships lowering their buckets where they were in order to retrieve fresh water is a classic metaphor for the perceived necessity of a certain stasis within the Black American community, the staying put that was paradoxically necessary if blacks were ever to advance.[16] It is then an important attempt to narrate what Washington surely took to be the profundity of black racial distinctiveness, of black tradition. And though he is able to imagine a moment beyond a ridiculous and damaging black/white rivalry, he nonetheless is still not able to push beyond the idea of competing camps, social and identity formations so ancient and secure that their interactions must follow a script that neither has had a hand in writing.

My quarrel with Washington then and with the various intellectual tendencies that I believe he represents is again ethical and historical. Washington clearly did not understand that the farm- and craft-based society that he championed was rapidly declining. Thus the wheelwrights, blacksmiths, carpenters, and planters that he trained at Tuskegee would find themselves woefully underprepared for competition with their (white) peers. More significant still was the fact that the changes in technology that drove American industrialization also rather profoundly affected the ways in which all Americans would come to conceptualize their world and themselves. The railroad, the automobile, and the airplane would help break already tenuous connections to the land (as evinced by the migrations of Black Americans during the early part of the century), while the telephone, radio, television, and movie theater would effectively change normative conceptions of the body's own limits. What is this thing that we call race when "black" voices can be heard over Norwegian radios and "Asian" faces can be seen even in the dark movie houses of the segregated South? Thus what Washington could not have foreseen was that the new industrial order for which he was so poorly training his students was one that was, yes, caught up in the old racialisms of the nineteenth century but that also had embedded within it the contradictions that would typify our confusions over race in the twenty-first. As it became increasingly apparent that race was immaterial, it became that much more apparent that its maintenance was, in fact, a matter of the performance of individual and communal will, a matter of choice. I would add to this only that this choice was imagined by earlier generations of Americans as operating precisely on the terrain of desire and indeed of sexuality. In fact the country's gory history of lynching speaks to the profound fear that in the absence of severe policing, black and white individuals would choose, predictably enough, each other.

II

> In our society which is white—we are intruders they say—there has got to be something inherently horrible about having the sicknesses and weaknesses of that society described by a person who is victim of them; for if he, the victim, is capable of describing what they have believed nonexistent, then they, the members of the majority, must choose between living the truth, which can be pretty grim, and the lie, which isn't much better. But at least they will then have the choice.
> —John A. Williams, *The Man Who Cried I Am*

We turn again to the image with which we began our discussions, the image of the Black American intellectual, in one of Europe's great cities, startled as he faces bad news carried with him from home. In this instance, however, the scenes have been provided by John A. Williams, whose *roman à clef The Man Who Cried I Am* provides a truly remarkable account of the ethical dilemmas that Black American intellectuals of the postwar generation faced.[17] The novel opens with its protagonist, Max Reddick, sitting sick and alone on the Leidsplein in Amsterdam. The cancer that has seized his body causes him the greatest of pain during urination and requires that he continually replace a heavy wad of cotton, arranged inside his underwear in order to collect the pus and blood that his body constantly sheds. Williams, however, is less concerned with the fact of Max's dying than he is with a certain species of remembering and settling of accounts. The most significant formal feature of the *roman à clef* may be that as it represents the traditions of an already lost generation, it also offers a challenge to the next. It is a hail, a call from one intellectual to another, both perhaps alone at desks in borrowed European apartments.

What compels Max to return to Amsterdam, then, what forces him to seek refuge abroad, is that vertigo caused by his attempt to maintain allegiance to (Black American) community when he has, in fact, become aware that he might do otherwise, that he is, in a word, free. Thus Max attempts to reconcile nothing less than the weight of history with the reality of his own desires and needs as an individual. He returns to Amsterdam, therefore, with two goals in mind. First, he must act on the letter left to him by his friend and mentor, Harry Ames, a character modeled closely on Richard Wright. Second, he must care for both his ravaged body and his ravaged relationships in these final days. He must make amends, swallow pride, state with grace and humility that he is sorry.

The letter that Max carries with him, this long text presented from beyond the veil, continually reasserts itself in the novel, becoming for Williams the ugly truth against which all else must be measured. It is a text that not only disrupts the desires of Harry and Max but that also regularly interrupts the progression of the novel itself. Therein Harry details the efforts of *Alliance Blanc,* a coalition of nations, including France, Great Britain, Belgium, Portugal, Australia, Spain, Brazil, South Africa, and the United States, that have come together to squelch the drive toward independence and self-reliance clearly evident among the "colored peoples" of Africa, Asia, Latin America, Europe, and of course North America itself. For possessing this information, Harry is killed. Indeed he dies, like Wright, under a cloud of suspicion. He does, however, leave a copy of the letter with his white European lover, Michelle, who delivers it to Max, who subsequently reads it, over transatlantic telephone lines, to a (Malcolm X–inspired) Minister Q. This act precipitates Max's murder at the hands of an American intelligence agent. Indeed in the course of the novel all those persons who come into contact with this particularly toxic piece of prose meet untimely deaths. This includes not only Harry, Max, and Minister Q but also Jaja Enzkwu, a lusty

Nigerian diplomat (Nnamdi Azikiwe?), whose two passions are the deliverance of his people from the oppression of "the white man" and the deliverance of his own, dark, sweaty, and heavily perfumed body into the unbelievably welcoming arms of "the white woman."

It is this same Jaja, the Jaja who is met with ridicule throughout the novel, the Jaja who is described as "eagle-faced, hot-eyed . . . with sweaty, pussy-probing fingers and perfumed agbadas" (Williams, 362), who first uncovers the truth of the *Alliance Blanc* and their King Alfred Plan, a blueprint for squelching black insurgency by turning to those grotesque methods of confinement and internment utilized by the Germans—and the Americans—a scant two decades earlier. Thus one is forced to the conclusion that it is Jaja, with those sweaty, pussy-probing fingers, who stood most solidly at that difficult location that I have argued the Black American intellectual must continually inhabit. His personal desires, the desires of a man who is not particularly likeable or even remarkable, are not eclipsed by his responsibility to community. Instead in Jaja's case it is impossible to distinguish individual drive from communal need. Jaja becomes suspicious, in fact, when he sees large numbers of government representatives gathering in San Sebastian in the Basque Country during the cold Basque winter. Jaja was himself at this summer resort in the dead of winter in order to pursue a potential lover. Indeed he would continue this rather stunningly common tendency to tether sex to politics until his own death in Basel in the hotel room of a startled, and yet to be ravished, Baroness. Or, as Williams would have it, "Jaja died as he had lived, chasing white pussy" (367).

Thus by the end of Williams's long novel one is left with the sense that drifting rather prominently in the deadly wake of the information contained in Harry's letter are women, *white* women, desire for whom acts both to drive and contain revolutionary fervor. We have at the center of a story about Black American intellectuals not only Jaja and his Baroness but also Harry and both his lover, Michelle, and wife, Charlotte, not to mention Max and his many lovers (thus that red dick). All, moreover, men and women alike, are heavily involved, innocently and not so innocently, nobly and with tragedy nipping at their heels, in the "getting and giving of pussy" all "in the name of the Negro Cause" (46). The upshot is of course that among the many things that the war does is to unsettle many of the traditional structures that held together the modern West. Or to state the matter with a bit more precision, the shocking realities of World War II made it clear that many of our most cherished, most sacred traditions were at best sophisticated means by which to discipline desire and at worst simple hokum. Thus all that "getting and giving of pussy" functioned as a sort of deep play. Black and white participants were of course eager to act upon the new social freedoms that came about after the war. At the same time, however, their fascination with one another, their sense of entering new territory, of coming into close proximity with "the other," continued the clumsy logic that their distinctions were not only real but profound. Thus even though their lovemaking and their energetic attempts at disgracing their families or shocking the odd Basque concierge should have had the effect of demonstrating common humanity, it all too often worked to reiterate a sort of metaphysics of difference in which black and white, man and woman were no more peculiar, no more separate than when they stood naked, one in front of the other. But then, of course, there is Margrit.[18]

Max Reddick sits alone on the Leidsplein in Amsterdam, a dangerous letter from a dead friend weighing down his briefcase, an uncomfortable, pus-filled wad of cotton resting heavily in his underwear. He sips Pernod and waits for his wife, Margrit. It is Margrit, alone among the many characters whom Williams presents, who understands fully the routes of her desire. She understands, perhaps as well as anyone can, the odd trick of history that casts an alluring cloud of mystery over her Black American husband. She understands when she looks at him, frail and afraid, hand shaking as he sets a half-finished glass of Pernod on the table, that her love is somehow inextricably caught up with the memory of a "big, ponderously walking Negro who led a column of liberating black Americans through the streets of Groningen" (Williams, 27–28). She understands when she looks into Max's brown face that her feeling for this man carries with it something of a childhood memory of chocolate bars, tiny American flags, and an end to deprivation. She also understands, however, that it is this same history (this same desire) that has driven them apart.

Max himself was one of those valiant black men who helped liberate a suffering Europe. And like his comrades, he came back changed, uncomfortably aware of the ugly commingling of compassion and violence that stands at the heart of modern subjectivity. Max simply cannot forget. He cannot forget either the deprivations that he suffered in the segregated army unit that he led or the deprivations that he caused. More importantly he cannot forget his own capacity for cruelty. He cannot forget leading a column into an Italian village, the black, blue, yellow, brown faces of his squad causing a stir among the timid population of women and children. He cannot forget his comrade, Barnes, who broke away from the squad in order to pursue "some pussy" in a house where young and old women had taken refuge. He cannot forget the sound of the explosion, Barnes's grenades ripping apart as they destroyed the upper floor of the building, all in the name of "takin' no chances." He cannot forget his own quick, mechanical reactions as he brought the butt of his carbine down on the side of the corporal's jaw, breaking it, nor the ugly sound of his own voice as he ordered one of his men to "help him along" (82–84). But most importantly, he cannot forget his attempts at forgetting, the desperate manner of his own repression.

She wanted to know his name, this fat Italian girl, hungry for food and affection. But Max had experienced too much of war to be bothered with sentimentality. He answers, "Joe." He wanted sex, not love, cruel animal dominance leading perhaps to life, not stupid gestures of a common humanity that might leave one dead. Max Reddick had become something different, hurt and oddly self aware, a killing machine looking for a way out of the trap of an irrepressible blood lust. He plunged brutally into the woman, satisfying something strange and frightening within himself, then withdrew, pulled up his pants and pressed a wad of bills into her fat hand. He was satisfied. Indeed the change had come.

> He turned to urinate and the woman about to leave, saw. "*Sangue!*" she hissed and, holding her stomach as if it had been polluted, ran out of the building. Jesus, Max thought, watching the blood come out in a dark ugly stream. Blood, how about that? I've got jaundice. Jaundice? Jaundice! . . . He replaced his helmet and snatched his carbine and ran out of the building. . . . He ran a few steps then bounded into the air shouting, "CALDONIA, CALDONIA, WHAT MAKES YOUR BIG HEAD SO HARD? MOPPPP!" Breathless, he came across his squad. . . . "Look, you bastards," Max cried. He took out his penis and urinated for them. "See that? That's blood. Jaundice. I'm out of this shit, make it on your own." He took off his helmet and . . . sent it whining off the wall of a house. That was the ritual for the man wounded enough to get out of it for good. (87–88)

One sees then that Max and Barnes are not so dissimilar. The truth of the matter is that just like Jaja with his baroness, the two men when confronted with the obvious humanity of the white "other" find themselves incapable of conceding the old rivalries. For to do so would not only force the question of their own freedom of choice, even within the most horrendous situations, but also it would throw into disarray the basic structures of their desire. That is to say, how can a modern black man take a contemporary white woman to bed after the specters of danger, trespass, defilement, and retribution have been thrown out? Indeed if there are no complex structures of tradition underwriting the attraction of the pink to the brown then one might very well lose hold of the erotic charge that gets one into the occasional Italian barn in the first place.

Max Reddick is indeed wounded as he sits on the Leidsplein across from his wife. But of course it is not jaundice nor cancer nor even the ugly memory of war that has produced the wound. Instead what bothers him, what is killing him, is the recognition that he is, in fact, not different from other men. Even within a life circumscribed by racist oppression one continues in one's freedom. Max has had to choose between right and wrong, and he has not always chosen correctly. Thus what weighs even more heavily than these ugly memories or that letter from Harry or that wet and uncomfortable wad of cotton is the fact that he has become almost too perfectly American. Those moments of victimization that he has suffered and those that he has inflicted have not been allowed to stand. Nor have they, it seems, been properly repressed. Instead they have been shorn of all meaning, forced into a sugary narrative that removes the individual from the realm of responsibility.

When Max returns from the war he resumes his career as a journalist and novelist, publishing a recollection of his time in Europe. The Italian girl makes a reappearance but this time as a young, innocent peasant with whom the valiant, if benighted, Black American soldier has fallen in love. His novel ends not with hiked skirt, bloody urine, nor even discarded helmet but instead with white MPs discovering the pair in a barn, killing them, and then covering their bodies with horse manure (Williams, 89). That is to say, Max allows his own narrative, the reality of his existence, to be turned to shit.

Williams is relentless in this refusal of the sentimentalism that is often attached to things black and American. Not only does he regularly lampoon revered black activists and intellectuals: Richard Wright, James Baldwin, Chester Himes, Martin Luther King, and Malcolm X, among others, but he also holds the reader's feet to the fire, as it were, suggesting that the very fact of the intellectual's self-reflection, the fact that he is the subject who might most easily come to question his society's most cherished beliefs and conceits and perhaps even reject them, produces him as an odd, potentially dangerous figure. More specifically, Williams is extremely sensitive to the reality that the crisis of the intellectual, Negro or otherwise, always takes place at the point at which the desires of the individual conflict with the presumed needs of the community. Or to turn the matter on its head, Black American intellectualism might be understood simply as that incessant mapping of the conflict between personal and communal desire. Indeed the struggle to establish a stable Black American identity is not simply political but also personal and erotic.

I would submit then that what troubles Williams is the fact that he understands all too clearly the pettiness of our desire. The difficulty that Williams narrates, our deeply American "problem," is not that we value our eroticism, our pleasure, too little but, on the contrary, too much. We have established a fake profundity around questions of desire. We have created this obscene creature, racial desire, and we have insisted that even though one might see its modernity quite clearly, we must nonetheless approach it as if it is the most ancient of beasts. But, as with the assorted dragons, unicorns, zephyrs, trolls, and bogeymen of our youth, one eventually must come to face directly the anxieties that these creatures represent if one is ever to enter into the fullness of human subjectivity.

It should come as no surprise that the emblematic figure for Williams, in this regard, is the homosexual, that subject who produces his (and the homosexual is almost always a man in these pages) intellectualism precisely by removing himself from commonsensical notions of tradition and societal responsibility. By refusing the imperative of procreation, the imperative to reproduce family and race, Williams's homosexual allows himself the freedom necessary to critically *disengage* from his society, to fashion a modern intellectualism, one no longer forced to bear the burden of tradition. Desire is unleashed, and in this way the modern subject comes to understand that his choices, erotic and otherwise, are precisely and undeniably *his* choices, not the reiteration of a set of narratives and beliefs that come to him from out of antiquity. Thus there is a way in which one might recognize all modern intellectualism as intimately caught up with homosexual subjectivity or what we have come to call "queerness."[19] Harry Ames himself is confronted with just this reality after hearing that his enemies have started a rumor that he has been passed over for a fellowship from the "Lykeion" because he is not only a radical but also a "queer." Tellingly, the distinction between radical and queer becomes difficult for Harry himself to maintain:

Is Harry Ames a faggot? . . . He felt as though a great many people had defecated on him. He wanted to strike out, but he knew if he did, he would not stop until he had killed. . . . I don't want to have to kill someone. I don't want to kill. Well, Paris would be different. Paris, and, if everything went all right, Africa. His friend Jaja Enzkwu from Nigeria had sent him a note of consolation on the Lykeion incident. "In our new, bright world, Africa, brother, we will have to ask them for nothing. It is a prospect that pleases me immensely. The Black Mother will forever beckon to her sons in the West. It is good that you plan to come home." (Williams, 137)

The level of irony at play in this passage is breathtaking. For though Harry Ames, like Richard Wright, escaped the confines of the United States, presumably to shore up an abused black masculinity, he makes that escape to Paris, a city that in the American imagination is altogether caught up with notions of decadence and profligacy. Moreover, he takes solace from his friend Jaja Enzkwu, who writes beautifully of the "Black Mother . . . beckon[ing] to her sons in the West." Jaja himself, however, was most likely to have written this letter while his white lover beckoned to him from the other side of a European hotel room.

The truth of the matter, therefore, is that Harry's enemies may not have been so far off the mark. An important, if too infrequently noted, fact of American history is that the same forces that drove millions of Black Americans to cities like New York, Chicago, and San Francisco both before and after World War II also encouraged scores of homosexuals, of all shades and both sexes, to make the same journey. Again we see that basic changes in the *social* structure of society allow for quite significant shifts in the deep ideological structures of that same society. I would argue, moreover, that the policing of these two presumably distinct communities operated in remarkably similar ways. The black and the homosexual could be tolerated if they remained out of sight, if they did not, so to speak, "flaunt it." In the case of the homosexual, this meant that one could demonstrate same-sex affection only within the most restricted of arenas, the so-called gay ghetto. As for the black, he could only be tolerated among whites if he wore the stamp of the (guest) worker. This logic is completely thrown into disarray, however, when the black worker walks hand-in-hand down the street with his white lover. Indeed, as scores of American autobiographers of the 1950s and 1960s have informed us, police officers all over the country were often hostile, but they turned absolutely vicious when they came into contact with either the homosexual or the interracialist. I would only add to this that what the policeman confronts when he sees our workers-cum-interracialists is the vertigo caused when one is confronted by the fact that the structures of desire are not nearly so stable as had been previously imagined. Once you go black who knows what else happens.

This is all constantly on the mind of Max Reddick, who not only must come to terms with his inability to maintain any stable heterosexual relationship, as evinced by his white wife's leaving him on the day of the famed 1963 March on Washington, but also with the reality that his own quite successful career was given great assistance by a white flamboyantly homosexual (Carl Van Vechtenesque) Granville Bryant. I should note that though Max Reddick is an altogether original character, his "biography" is reminiscent of that of the infinitely macho Chester Himes, who maintained a remarkably close relationship with Van Vechten throughout much of his life.[20] This then is why Max dreams (during a hospitalization to remove troublesome hemorrhoids) that Bryant comes to visit him and reveals that homosexuals are, in fact, not of this earth but are a race of superior men who crash landed on the planet many thousands of years ago and who have ever since been carefully insinuating themselves into centers of power. It is unclear, moreover, whether they intend to recruit Max to their cause or to inform him that he is one of these "outer-space" men himself, hopelessly lost to the realities of everyday life and the call of race pride (see Williams, 188–190). Williams's genius here turns on the fact that he suggests that the structures of desire might change so drastically that the old rigid lines of communication between man and woman, black and white might be put to altogether novel uses. At the same time Max's dream suggests that underlying what are taken to be perhaps old-fashioned, "profound" ways of conceptualizing and articulating desire is a set of edicts and prescriptions, all designed to gain and enforce control over undisciplined subjectivity.

It is this very strain between tradition-bound desire and a certain queer pleasure that fuels Max's rather obsessive interest in the figure of Moses Boatwright, a character whose name "called up the image of a tall, rangy negro farmer dressed in faded overalls, in the Deep South, standing astride a cotton patch, a shaggy felt hat pulled low on his head to beat back the sun" (52), but who was, in fact, a student of philosophy, a Harvard graduate, and most importantly a celebrated, if unlikely, cannibal who had killed a white delivery man, stored his body in a basement refrigerator, and eaten pieces from it at his leisure. Nowhere in the novel does Williams present a clearer example of the difficulty that he and Max (or is it the whole of America?) have in distinguishing the Negro from the sexual pervert. When confronted with the sensation that the Boatwright story has created, Max comments,

> It did not matter that the police blotter could read about a woman who had had love made to her by her dog so that her shoulders, buttocks and back were covered by deep scratches; it was really no concern of his that two men had been hospitalized, under guard, still together like dogs, one imbedded so deeply in the other that one had died and that the live one, still nude, tragedy roughly overriding their perversion, cried and hid his face; could he even bother to finish reading what one lesbian had done to another with her teeth and where? Bother with murders and beatings, why? When it was all said and done, the only clean job a cop could enjoy perhaps was the one where the enemy had but a single perversion—color. (54)

It is an easy enough matter for me to remind my readers of the arguments that I have made already, easy enough to reiterate the fact that for the (white) police officer the image of a black hand inside a white one is indistinct from images of sharp-toothed lesbians, white women who are a bit too animal friendly, or male homosexual couples that somehow mutate into monstrous singularities. I would maintain, however, that by stopping with these observations one would squander an opportunity to make sense of why it is that Williams has chosen to create such a thick layer of potent, if unlikely, imagery. The inevitable logic with which we are confronted is not so much that the black, the Negro, the colored is always thought to be more prone to sexual perversion but instead that blackness itself, that telltale color, is always a sort of sexual crime regardless of how it is articulated. The presence of the black in *any* location represents precisely the failure of American and European eugenicist projects, a failure that has occurred because the black is not only threatening but appealing, not only the monster that the policeman must beat into submission but also the beauty without whom he cannot seem to live.

Thus the great difficulty for the Black American intellectual is not, as many would suggest, that we have had to arrange ourselves between seemingly incommensurate poles, that we have had to negotiate a terrain in which our countrymen—and women—have denied us the ability to walk unhampered down the street during the brightest part of the day while begging our favors in the dead of night. On the contrary, our difficulty, indeed some would say our shame, is that we have negotiated this terrain so very well. Once you go black, you never go back. The myth of our potent sexuality has been, I would argue, not only a great burden but also one of the most potent means by which we have resisted—or at least adapted—racist and racialist oppression. This resistance turns, moreover, on our ability to cleverly rearticulate the very logic of an ancient and profound distinction between black and white that stands behind all of the ugly racialism for which our proud nation is so famous. The great crime of Moses Boatwright then is not that he cuts out the heart and genitals of a white man and eats them but instead that he comes to embrace fully the contradiction that is his life; he recognizes that no matter how refined his intellect, when he enters a room perversion (and the inevitable attraction to that perversion) enters with him. In doing so, however, in accepting the conditions of his existence, he does escape the strictures of American racialism; that is to say, he chooses.

> I was born seeing precisely, Mr. Reddick. There *were* times when I chose too. Death, for example. A man would like to pick the way he wants to die. In bed in his sleep, mostly. By my acts I decided how I would die. But those acts had more in them. This world is an illusion, Mr. Reddick, but it can be real. I went prowling on the jungle side of the road where few people ever go because there are things there, crawling, slimy, terrible things that always remind us that down deep we are rotten, stinking beasts. Now, because of what I did, someone will work a little harder to improve the species. (58–59)

It is important, I believe, that I point out again the well-established maxim that though the human subject possesses the ability to choose, his choice is always conditioned by his society. More significant still is the fact that though one possesses freedom of choice, this does not mean that one will choose correctly. This is, in fact, the very essence of freedom. Thus the modern subject, the subject who is confronted with the reality of his freedom, is always met by a profound ethical dilemma. The ability to break with the strictures of society may require that one become not simply an outsider, as it were, but also a monster, a destroyer, the very beast that one's society most fears.

It is perhaps not so odd then that so many of the intellectuals to whom we will reintroduce ourselves in this study struggled not so much against the racialism of American society as within it. They clearly believed that a break with society, even a society as grotesquely racist as the United States, would involve not only a break with the oppressor but also, in a sense, a break with the humdrum, sanitized self. As Moses Boatwright sets down to a delicious meal of heart and balls, he may be free, but it is a freedom not only from white racism but also from family, friends, community, indeed every aspect of "civilized" life. Thus it seems strange that we have seen so much revolutionary rhetoric in contemporary American society, for if, in fact, revolution should come to these United States, it would no doubt spell not simply the end to white racism but to blackness and Black American identity as well.

The pages that follow will be divided into two sections. In the first, "Going Black," we will look at the late novels of the three most prominent Black American writers of the mid-twentieth century: Richard Wright, Ralph Ellison, and James Baldwin. I will suggest that each of these works is similar to that of Williams in that they reject the notion of the black as innocent and instead insist upon his modernity and thus responsibility within modern society. In so doing they challenge notions of an already decided black identity. Indeed one of the ways they advance the tradition of Black American writing is that they turn their attention away from the presumably static cultures of the folk and toward the complicated narratives of urban, cosmopolitan, sophisticated blacks. They attempt to break open the trap of innocence and primitivism that they believe too heavily burdens the Black American. They suggest in their works that black identity, if it is to exist at all, must be chosen by contemporary generations of Americans. And more to the point, if blackness is to have any future at all, then so-called black intellectuals must create modes of black articulation that do not turn on the erroneous assumption of profound racial distinction.

In the second section, "Coming Back?" I will examine a number of rather complicated responses to this presumed erosion of Black American innocence, this destruction of black profundity. In particular, I will pay special attention to articulations of black masculinity by Huey Newton, one of the two founders of the Black Panther Party, and filmmaker Melvin Van Peebles, director of the classic film *Sweet Sweetback's Baadasssss Song*, whose careers, I will argue, strangely overlap the two tendencies within black intellectualism that I am attempting to represent here. This second tendency among

Black American intellectuals works specifically to resist the possibility of an amoral Black American identity formation as evinced by a character like Boatwright. Moreover, in each of the texts that I examine, I will argue that we see an almost desperate attempt to reestablish a quickly disarticulating Black American identity precisely by reworking the tropes of innocence and profundity that had been so seriously thrown into disarray by Wright, Ellison, and Baldwin. Finally, I will argue throughout *Once You Go Black* that we ought never to allow our understandings of black and American traditions to become so precious that we forget to consider seriously the questions of freedom of choice, patriotism, individual and communal responsibility that are the very substance of contemporary culture and politics.

Going Black

1

The Funny Father's Luck

I am eager to burn this threadbare masculinity
This perpetual black suit
I have outgrown.

—Essex Hemphill, "Heavy Breathing"

Once You Go Black is concerned with individual intellectuals, their works, the *reception* of their works, their biographies, and indeed the *reception* of their biographies. Or to put the matter more straightforwardly still, *Once You Go Black* greedily partakes in a suspect, if not altogether outmoded, literary historical method built around great men and their great books. One might rightly argue then that this work looks not so much old-fashioned as antique. One of the things that shocks even its author is how closely the text hews to narratives of American literary and cultural history that parallel the life histories of "representative men," those famed American intellectuals who came of age after the last of the great wars and who quickly redirected the main currents of American life and letters.

Still, I hope it is clear that what I am attempting here is precisely *not* to continue what might be thought of as the common sense of Black American literary and cultural criticism. I am not concerned with recounting the noble story of a noble people as demonstrated by the fine example of mid-twentieth-century black intellectuals. This is even while I might readily acknowledge the necessity of such projects. What motivates this study, however, is the concern that all too often students of Black American literature and culture reproduce notions of a stagnant Black American history by insisting that the anguished cries of the slave are ultimately indistinct from the complicated musings of the contemporary artist. Thus I emphasize individualism and peculiarity in these pages not simply to privilege creative singularity and independence but instead to remind my readers that much of what we take to be inevitable (the nature of desire) is at once chosen and historically contingent.[1]

I

I say all of this as a preamble to my invocation of the name Richard Wright, the putative father of contemporary Black American literature. Wright was not unexpectedly an inadequate parent, the man who allowed his own individualism, his perverse desire, to sever the necessary, life-sustaining link between "the (black) self" and the traditions that presumably sustain it. In doing so, Wright showed that the structures of desire that should tether an artist to his people are ultimately constructed through only partially acknowledged notions of black fidelity and consanguinity. Worse yet, Wright demonstrated in the most graphic manner possible (his literal and figurative expatriation) that one might, if not properly policed, leave off with one's affirmations of racial distinctiveness, stop one's black talk. Thus those intellectuals who follow in Wright's wake are invited to begin nothing less than the difficult, clumsy process of establishing a vocabulary of race and racialism that is not already known, not already familiar within the traditions of black/white conflict that Americans hold so dear.

One might easily see then how Wright and the many other American intellectuals whom I take him to represent could be recognized as funny. When the so-called black intellectual announces his peculiar gifts, when he suggests that his ideas, his methods, his styles borrow from and add to the richest and deepest veins of "our" traditions, he necessarily demonstrates the clumsy, yet doggedly alive, discourses of race, class, gender, and sexuality that radically structure the standards by which we deem individuals fit for celebration and publicity. Thus Richard Wright, standing as he does at the front of the line, the father of modern Black American literature, perhaps the finest Negro novelist of the twentieth century, could not be anything less than a suspect figure. One might, in fact, boil down the variety of questions that cascade over the enigma of Wright to just one: "If he is so Negro, how then could he be such a writer? Funny, isn't it?"

I want to be careful to stress that I am not after the same type of unmasking of Richard Wright that novelist Margaret Walker attempts in her 1988 biography, *Richard Wright: Daemonic Genius.*[2] Though I find this work compelling, I do recognize that Walker's treatment of Wright is often over the top, suggesting as she does that Wright was not only bisexual but also paranoid, shy, naive, puritanical, *and* homophobic. Nonetheless, I think that the shock that meets Walker's efforts, whether one appreciates them or not, stems from our irritation at both the unseemliness of her concern with the petty, grimy details of the master's life as well as the fact that her efforts unsettle normative rhetorics of Black American intellectualism, rhetorics that turn on notions of the Black American's deep southern roots, his intimate connection to the folk, his honesty, his wholesome political and social engagement, his childlike innocence, his "blackness." I would add to this that these strategies for the narration of the black intellectual have the effect of further obscuring any notion of black sexual agency, the black as mature sexual subject. Within the unchanging erotic narrative that one conjures with but a single word, "Mississippi," the Black American not only has a decidedly limited variety of roles to play (victim or witness), but also he seems to have always played them already. His is the ultimate twice-told story. "Oh yes quite fine now. But remember he came from down South."

I am attempting here to develop the idea of the funny intellectual as a corollary and counterpart to the notion of the queer intellectual. I want to resist the assumption that the funniness that I ascribe to Wright might be understood as a simple stand-in for some simplistic version of queerness. That is to say, funniness does not only or even primarily suggest masked homoeroticism or repressed homosexuality. Instead I would suggest that "funny" stands before queer precisely to the extent that it has the ability to delay consideration of mature (sexual) subjectivity. Thus I will reiterate my suspicion that part of Wright's genius was his ability to map narratives of intellectual celebrity in such a way that the presumably "queer" aspects of his personality, those many parts of his persona that encroached upon "sexual abnormality," were channeled into familiar narratives of youthful experimentation. Indeed a rather strange duality becomes apparent when examining Wright and his work. All of the most interesting characteristics of the mature intellectual—his politics, his aesthetics, his relationship to community, his sexuality—are understood as the ultimate result of the particular pressures he faced as a black youth. In a sense then Richard Wright is never allowed to grow up, no matter what dates may have been printed inside his passport. Thus his searing critique of American society could be heard precisely as the funny protests of a brilliant, if overly idealistic, child. Whether as a youth from Mississippi, a migrant from Chicago, a bohemian from New York, or even, I would venture, an expatriate in Paris, Wright managed during much of his career to remain not only critical of but aloof from the mainstream precincts of American society. By doing so he was able to gain, one is led to believe, an innocent and essentially more honest perspective on the realities of America.

Again, strangely enough, the figure that haunts these pages is Booker T. Washington, whose articulation of a primary and necessary symbiosis between the Negro and the South has been roundly critiqued, roughly handled, sniffed at derisively, but still not quite set aside. On the contrary, one still finds even the most sophisticated students of American culture genuflecting toward a rather uncomplicated narrative of Black American migration (just think of all those southern grandmothers spoken of so fondly in Boston apartments). I submit, moreover, that Wright's deployment of this narrative works precisely to the extent that it enables the continuance of the traditional Negro, the old South. Indeed the notion of the essentially southern and rural origins of the Black American community continues as one of the last shibboleths of the (Black) American cultural mythos, not simply because of the historical realities of slavery and migration (realities that cannot themselves be neatly arranged on north/south, youth/adult axes) but also because of the manner in which it allows a comforting pastoralism to be snuck into otherwise sober, some might say dour, conceptions of modern subjectivity.

The oft-repeated tale of the Black American's southern identity has the effect of settling him in a territory outside both space and time. No matter those long years in Paris, Berlin, or New York, he is always a southern boy, so mannered, friendly, and open, so not like us. Thus even the hard-edged and perennially pessimistic Jean-Paul Sartre cannot help, it seems, but view his friend Wright as a sort of thinking man's primitive.

> Let us take the case of the great negro writer, Richard Wright. If we consider only his condition as a *man,* that is, as a Southern "nigger" transported to the North, we shall at once imagine that he can only write about Negroes or Whites *seen through the eyes of Negroes.* Can one imagine for a moment that he would agree to pass his life in the contemplation of the eternal True, Good, and Beautiful when ninety percent of the Negroes in the South are practically deprived of the right to vote? And if anyone speaks here about the treason of the clerks, I answer that there are no clerks among the oppressed.[3]

One feels while reading these lines a strange mixture of amusement and depression. It is not that Sartre assumes that Wright can only see through (disabled) Negro eyes. Indeed Sartre ultimately assumes a rather puzzling modesty here, suggesting that the Negro writer will by necessity see more clearly than his white counterpart. It is after all the Negro who recognizes those ninety percent of deprived southerners, while the white, alas, does not. I do feel compelled to ask, however, what has happened to Sartre's well-publicized sense of irony; which measures of human complexity left his consciousness on the day he first met Richard Wright? For is it not here, at the sign of the Negro, that Sartre abandons his own hard-won skepticism? Even as he writes passionately about Freedom, he demonstrates a profound unwillingness to abandon moral certainty. There are no Negro clerks. None. The idea itself is preposterous as clerks serve only the interests of the oppressors, and Negroes are most decidedly *the oppressed*. Still, I would argue that the evidence before us suggests that Sartre knew very little about Negroes and even less about clerks. His lapse in reasoning, his blackout, if you will, is demonstrated not only in the often less than salutary histories of both postcolonial Africa and desegregated America, histories in which clerks and Negroes are sometimes indistinguishable, but also in the person of Richard Wright himself.

I repeat, I am not accusing Richard Wright of being a clerk in existentialist clothing (though I must admit a guilty fascination with his desperate struggles to secure a position in the U.S. Postal Service). Instead I would point out simply that *all* the evidence in Wright's archive points to a man who understood clearly that neither Black American identity nor racialized oppression exempted one from participation in the maintenance—and *re-articulation*—of the main structures of society, including those structures that work to oppress oneself and one's community. An individual very well might "turn clerk," as it were, if that meant the difference between life and annihilation. Thus what I *am* accusing Richard Wright of is that most American of American pastimes, dissimulation. I believe that though part of what is on display in Sartre's articulation of Wright's innocence is old-fashioned primitivism, one can also discern the somewhat obscured, but still recognizable, contours of Wright's own well-honed strategies to narrate his celebrity, his status as public intellectual. What gets in the way, of course, is the fact that the categories of celebrity and intellectual are difficult to maintain one with the other. Indeed the danger that the so-called public intellectual most often faces is that he will inadvertently find himself becoming a sort of publicity intellectual, a subject whose work becomes overly dependent upon both commercially driven trends as well as an unsophisticated, suffocating relationship to tradition.

The longest period of Richard Wright's career, the period after his successes with *Native Son* and *Black Boy,* his public departure from the Communist Party, and of course his move to France is one that is generally described in terms of decline, a theme that we will take up in greater detail in chapter 3. This is though Wright continued to search out new narrative strategies in his writing and achieved, I believe, some of his greatest successes in the last decade of his life. Thus one is continually shocked by the *ad hominem* nature of the attacks on Wright's later essays, travel accounts, and most especially his "late" novels, all of which were widely criticized for lacking the immediacy of *Native Son* and *Black Boy.* Wright the emigrant, the existentialist, and the interracialist had, it seemed, traveled too far from his roots. By the time of *The Long Dream*'s publication in 1958, "brother" intellectuals saw fit to publicly lecture Wright about not only the quality of his writing but also the peculiar arrangements of his personal life. " 'The Long Dream' proves that Wright has been away too long," Saunders Redding laments. "He has cut the emotional umbilical cord through which his art was fed, and all that remains for it to feed on is the memory, fading, of righteous love and anger. Come back, Dick Wright, to life again!"[4]

It would be unfair to say that Wright did not resent or attempt to counter such insults. Still, what intrigues the student of Richard Wright is how little the great author himself did to disrupt the rhetorical strategies by which this form of critique is offered. There is a surprising paucity of materials by Wright that attempt to take into account the realities of the mature intellectual well beyond the success of *Native Son* and long since delivered from the harsher realities of Mississippi segregation. I would suggest then that the fault here is not with *The Long Dream* but instead with the refusal of Wright and the more generous critics of Wright to meet Redding on the very ground that he marked out himself. One might, in fact, simply concede Redding's most damaging points. No, Richard Wright did not create *The Long Dream* from material he gained living close by the lived realities of 1950s Mississippi, great bastion of liberal democracy that apparently it was. But of course the novel is not, in fact, concerned solely or even primarily with Mississippi-style reality. Instead the obvious obsession in the work is with the never quite realized dream of an American subjectivity, a dream no less vivid because it comes to a dreamer with a Paris address. More to the point, Wright's emigration, his dislocation, those many necessary and inevitable moments of solitude confronting the American pursuing his craft on the Île de France, is a *sustaining,* indeed central, part of the dream's architecture. Richard Wright to my knowledge never made any such bold or positive defense of his expatriation. Instead, Wright continued, even as he boldly took up the mantle of existentialism and liberal internationalism, to narrate his own life and, by extension, his aesthetic as emanating from the crucible of Mississippi. Or to state the matter from the opposite direction, Paris is significant in Wright's life history precisely to the extent that it is *not* Mississippi.

I do understand that my argument runs counter to the notion of Wright as both modernist and internationalist. I should say again, therefore, that not only do I believe Wright to be one of the most significant American novelists of the twentieth century but also that his theorizations of Black American identity and culture were not only ahead of their time but prescient. They operate, in fact, as inspiration for much of the striving evident in this work.

> The history of the Negro in America is the history of America written in vivid and bloody terms; it is the history of Western Man writ small. It the history of men who adjust themselves to a world whose laws, customs, and instruments of force were leveled against them. The Negro is America's metaphor.[5]

I will assume that I need not dwell at great length on the obvious resonance between Negroes who become metaphors and persons who have gone black and seem not to have returned. I have suggested several times already that one of the most potent means by which Americans articulate reconciliation is to suggest blackness as a human possibility open to everyone. All people, or at least all American people, *ought*, it seems, to go black. My resistance to this line of thought turns on the recognition that this celebratory articulation of "Negro identity" works to short-circuit our active consideration of Negro persons as agents of history. Metaphors are powerful tools, but they are tools nonetheless, utilized to create other tools, usually other metaphors. I would argue then that Wright's labored deployment of a rhetoric of "Western Man" should actually not be dismissed as simple chauvinism or misogyny. Instead the cascade of determinatives in this syntactic chain, Negro–America–Western–Man–Metaphor, is not possible within the confines of even a slightly more complicated conception of human subjectivity. Add one more significant element to the conceptual apparatus Negro–America–Western–Man–Woman–Metaphor, then the entire enterprise begins to unravel. "What Negroes! A man and a woman?!" Americans begin to conjure planetary realignments at such moments.

And lest I stand accused of equating social agency and cultural reproduction with heterosexuality, I should say that my interest remains not so much with the Negro's gender or his sexuality as with the simple matter of his *sociality*. Wright is meticulous in his depiction of a subject so spectacular in its transnational and transhistorical reach as to seem rather flat when one gets up close. The Negro shows up for all the vivid and bloody events, but the manipulation of laws, customs, and those all-important instruments of force is left to other folks. When one adds another Negro into the mix, however, when *the* Negro morphs into *those Negroes!* one is forced to consider the possibility of a Negro social world. That is to say, the terms *Negro* and *World* do not contradict one another. Instead each is an attempt to articulate the social itself. Thus I can easily imagine an alternative narrative ("What Negroes! A man and man?!") that shorn of its implicit heterosexism would have the same effect of placing one on notice as to the late hour for our continual re-articulation of the Black American Pastoral. I submit then that what rankles Wright's critics is not only the fact that he was somehow not the man of the people that his works (especially *Uncle Tom's Children, Native Son, Black Boy,* and *Twelve Million Black Voices*) presumably describe, not only that he seemed always to be keeping some part of himself private and sacred, but also that his efforts at narrating the private/public binary seem so very formal, flat, and indeed funny.

> *Epic*
> Margaret Walker is a talker
> When she came to town
> What she said put Ted in bed
> And turned Dick upside down.[6]

This verse, sent to Margaret Walker by Richard Wright following the collapse of their friendship during the Second American Writers Conference in June 1936, is a very funny piece of writing. While it is beyond my abilities to defend Wright as a poet, it is quite possible, I believe, for even the clumsiest reader to see that the Wright who sent these scandalously revealing lines to a newly minted enemy understood and desired (I am profoundly confused as to which came first) that this moment, the moment of the presumably "queer" reading of "personal" evidence left by a "public" intellectual, would indeed come. In fact, Wright sent the poem to Walker on a postcard, thus belying even the fiction of the private letter passed between intimates. The obvious work that this quick, witty poem does is to condense the details of Walker's falling out of favor with Wright and the community of artists gathered around him. The piece functions properly then to the extent that it denatures a bit of queer gossip, turns it funny, by subjecting it to the strict discipline of verse. The three rhymes—Walker/talker, town/down, Ted/bed—rehearse Walker's major talking points with such an impeccable air of dispassion that they become almost a mantra.[7] Thus it is easy enough to suggest that what Wright is after is a sort of poetics of gossip in which words only ever refer to other words. This does not quite explain, however, why one of the major elements of the poem is not so neatly paired as the others, not nearly so tightly wrapped. Indeed what has happened to Dick? Nothing rhymes with Dick?

There is an obvious cleverness on display here as Wright turns the tables on Walker by framing her as an unrepentant gossip while he himself continues the same scandalous line of narration that he ascribes to his erstwhile friend. Regardless of who said it, Ted is still in bed, and Dick is still inexplicably upside down. The displacement that takes place here, the routing of dangerous information through the safe harbor of (female) cattiness should seem altogether familiar to contemporary audiences. It is after all a device that has been used to great effect in American literature, allowing for the articulation of the most biting social critique. Moreover, the simple procedure that I am now demonstrating, my holding of the artifact up against a mirror fashioned with the precious metals of queer theory so that we might view better its (erotic) structure, should also seem familiar. Still, this does not exactly get at what I mean when I use the term *funny*. For while I must applaud any effort to recapture the "lost" narratives of sexuality imbedded in the varied histories of Black American intellectualism, I must also remain mindful of the incredible self-consciousness on display in these lines. I read this text as funny then precisely to the extent that it demonstrates Wright's quite efficacious procedures in his efforts to resolve tensions inherent in his status as a so-called marginal subject (if you walked in on him unexpectedly, you might just find him upside down) and what one might call his civility, that self-disciplining brought into play by his profound desire to speak not as a marginal, a queer, or even a black but as a representative American. In a sense, Wright wants it both ways. He wants his hard-won intellectual freedom as well as the ability to speak to and *for* his people. It is this tension between the profundity of the people's traditions and the superficiality, the phoniness, of the writers' ideas and techniques that I am attempting to mark as funny.

Funniness might be described then as one of the major technologies of publicity available to American intellectuals who produced their work in the years defined by World War II and its aftermath. It is clear to me, moreover, that one might name this technology in any number of ways. *Masking* and *passing* are the examples that come most readily to mind. My concern, however, is not with the matter of Wright's sex. Nor am I particularly eager to measure the quality of his "blackness." Instead what intrigues me is that Wright's funniness, this technology of publicity that he so deftly manipulated, ultimately establishes him neither as potential "sexual minority," ripe for the queering, nor even as a suspect Black American. Instead Wright's funniness is intriguing precisely to the extent that it is built upon a sort of awkward, childlike Black American civility, one that, in Wright's case, is caught between the Scylla of anti-Communism and the Charybdis of engaged intellectualism.

What the great black father of American literature wants is to free himself from the ordinary American binaries of left/right, black/white, male/female. At the same time he wants to hold on to that all-important fatherhood. He wishes to distance himself from "the commonsensical" within American life while seeming somehow not to be doing so at all; that is to say, he establishes himself as the Mississippian abroad. I am speaking now of course to the matter of Wright's many contradictions. But in so doing, I do not mean just to read the man and his work as having been (oh, well, ah) compromised but to suggest that these same compromises with art, politics, and community would, in fact, be modeled by an entire generation of American intellectuals, a generation whose own lively intellectual practices are themselves structured upon that childlike funniness suggesting innocence of which Wright himself was such a prominent architect.

Perhaps I can bring my thinking more clearly into focus by pointing out that the Second American Writers Conference, where Wright and Walker parted company, represented one of the last gasps of a publicly active Marxist (and especially Communist) Left in the United States. The sessions were dominated by news, all bad, from the Spanish Civil War, where the introduction of troops and equipment from Germany and Italy, along with the benign neglect of the United States, assured the victory of Franco's forces over the Loyalists. The even more frustrating reality, however, was that though American leftists were uniform in their support of Republican Spain, even sending the awkwardly named Abraham Lincoln Brigade to fight on the Spanish front, they nonetheless were in the throws of intense political and ideological upheaval. The rise to power in the Soviet Union of Stalin and the subsequent purges of Communists for what looked surprisingly like intellectual independence drove a deep wedge between those Americans who supported Stalin and the Soviets and those, like Wright, who had begun already to doubt.

Thus the question that Wright earnestly answered on the form given him by conference organizers, "Are you for, or are you against Franco and fascism? Are you for, or are you against the legal government and the people of Republican Spain?" revealed more than a zealous desire to marshal the talents and energies of American intellectuals for the good fight against fascism and for democracy.[8] Indeed the difficulty here is that both the question and the answer seem to be "yes." What is demonstrated by the enforced solipsism evident in this document is nothing less than the infantilization that continues even today to dog American intellectuals. Wright's response, "I am wholeheartedly and militantly pro-Loyalist and for the national freedom of the people of Spain," sounds strangely similar to those many wide-eyed statements made by a great many Americans, including Wright, regarding their deep and abiding disdain for Communists, Communism, and the variety of "queers" associated with the entire Queer/Commie enterprise.[9] Wright is then a perfectly civil character, one who is altogether prepared to make the correct gestures in order not to handicap his efforts to be heard in the public sphere, even and especially, I would add, that most corny and canonical gesture of utilizing the public ridicule of the female and the feminine as a sort of prologue to one's own entry onto the public stage. Wright is then rather like the atheist at Thanksgiving dinner who if he does not speak to God during the ritual prayers at least has the good sense to bow his head.

We return then to that funny poem sent to Margaret Walker. These five lines suggest finally of Wright that he is funny but not queer, a fine distinction perhaps but one that neatly parallels hislater role in the anti-Communist Left, both American and Continental. I would argue further that the fact of the poem's title, "Epic," alerts us to Wright's sense of writing himself—and Walker for that matter—into a historical narrative structured by the great efforts of great men, narrative that nonetheless supercedes these efforts. More important still, it demonstrates Wright's keen understanding of an increasingly rigid grammar of American civility. That is to say, the funny intellectualism that Wright allowed himself was produced precisely through the vehicle of his rather public capitulation to what he himself must have regarded as terribly outmoded narratives by which the intellectual might narrate his own celebrity. From child to adult, south to north, woman to man, or even primitive to modern, all of these narratives of the intellectual's development are rendered suspect in Wright's work, even as he repeatedly returns to them in his efforts to establish his audience.

II

> [It] seems that the contemporary Negro novelist and the dead New England woman are locked together in a deadly, timeless battle; the one uttering merciless exhortations, the other shouting curses. And, indeed, within this web of lust and fury, black and white can only thrust and counter-thrust, long for each other's slow, exquisite death; death by torture, acid, knives and burning; the thrust, the counter-thrust, the longing making the heavier that cloud which blinds and suffocates them both, so that they go down into the pit together.
>
> —James Baldwin, "Everybody's Protest Novel"

Richard Wright's last published novel, *The Long Dream,* is to my mind his most interesting, most accomplished work, though it is infrequently taught, haphazardly read, and more damning still, out of print.[10] When I say that it is Wright's most accomplished novel I mean to suggest that it is also Wright's most fatalistic. It is not à la Baldwin a work in which the mature author returns to his roots and accepts his native land on a set of negotiated terms that if not perfect are at least workable. Instead I would produce a sort of backwards précis of Wright's literary biography in which the starkness and coldness of *Native Son* would be taken as evidence of the fact that early Wright, Wright who was still producing his work within the confines of the Communist Party, very much believed—or wanted to believe—that the American project could be salvaged, that a young, poor, and poorly educated black writer from Mississippi might create a work so shocking, so absolutely real and unrelenting that the country would be forced to shake off centuries of lethargy, take hold of itself, and become nothing less than a modern democratic republic, one in which the simple matter of which color of hand might caress which shade of breast would not be so overdetermined as to threaten the norms of civility.

Indeed one of the most significant conceits of this chapter is the belief that there is, in fact, a great deal to be gained by reading Wright in both "early" and "late" phases. While I will take my own council in this matter and not attempt an explication of some essential difference between an apprentice and a mature Wright, I will suggest that it is naive to imagine that Wright was not burdened in his later work with precisely the fact of that publicity and celebrity with which we have been so much concerned. He is identified after *Native Son* as the father of modern (Black) American literature, and for better or worse that identification became part of the very discursive universe of which Wright was himself a master technician. Indeed Baldwin's figuration of Wright as a sort of heteroerotic racial combatant actually reiterates Wright's status as progenitor. I would suggest, in fact, that the venom so apparent in Baldwin's description, all that thrusting and counterthrusting, death by torture, acid, knives, *and* burning effectively rips away the last remnants of sentimentalism surrounding Wright and Stowe and delivers the couple up as a rather surprisingly well-matched heterosexual dyad. Moderns to the end, with equal portions of determination, they set themselves to the task of getting down into that pit together without all the long-windedness and purplish prose of previous generations.

Thus Baldwin's critique of Wright and Stowe had the effect of closing a long-open circuit in the conceptualization of American literary history. If Stowe was able in the nineteenth century to pull off a truly impressive spectacle of immaculate conception and reproduction (simultaneously giving birth to *Uncle Tom's Cabin* and, as George Eliot suggests, the tradition of the Negro Novel itself), she most certainly was not able to repeat her performance in the twentieth.[11] The longing that Hortense Spillers and others remark so ably in Stowe's text, the irrepressible desire for that most persistent and most old-fashioned of American taboos, the pairing of black man and white woman, is difficult I believe for even the sleepiest of Stowe's contemporary readers to miss.[12] Thus the new level of critical sophistication that Baldwin helps to bring into being forces one to the conclusion that all that timeless, deadly battling has its consequences. I will suggest then that if Richard Wright and Harriet Beecher Stowe were, in fact, in battle, that if they had succeeded as Baldwin seems to suggest in establishing a stability, a permanence in the erotic encounter between black and white, then perhaps one might read Wright's late text as the issue of all that exhorting and cursing, thrusting and counterthrusting. If *Uncle Tom's Cabin* is the bastard child of the white woman and *Native Son* that of the black man, then perhaps *The Long Dream* is the progeny of both, a final attempt at familial reconciliation.

Rex "Fishbelly" Tucker, the protagonist of *The Long Dream,* is clearly designed as the mirror opposite of Bigger (the doomed protagonist of *Native Son*). Whereas Bigger lives in grinding poverty, Fishbelly lives in black bourgeois luxury. He is teased by other children for the careful way in which he is dressed. His parents value his education, and he severely disappoints them when he drops out of high school. He is nonetheless rewarded with a new automobile as he becomes the business partner of his father, Tyree. The elder man has established himself as one of the most powerful individuals in town through his funeral home, rental properties, and houses of prostitution. That is to say, he deals in both hot and cold meat. Rex, never quite a king but still a prince of sorts, is a man who ought to be able to take control of his destiny in a manner that was clearly not allowed Bigger. He is not a refugee on the cold streets of Chicago but a true Mississippian, reared in the heat and violence of a region that by all rights should offer him a very promising future. "Son, see that long line of light?" Tyree says to Fish, seated beside him in a handsome car above the town of Clintonville.

> That's King Street and it divides the white folks from the black folks. All the town to the left of King Street's *our* town. The rest is white. Now, Clintonville's got about 25,000 folks, 15,000 of 'em's white, and 10,000 of 'em's black. That black part's your kingdom, son. We got everything there and you can have all the fun you want. (Wright, 148)

Wright's return to Mississippi in this late novel, published four years after the Supreme Court's 1954 *Brown v. Topeka Board of Education* decision, might easily have been understood as the exiled author's attempt to return himself if not to America then to an engaged writing project that was not only critical but also utilitarian. Indeed one of the ways Wright provokes the reader is to redirect attention precisely to the project of the reproduction of black patriarchy and paternity, the very subject that so perplexed the generation of intellectuals who followed in his wake. In so doing, however, Wright utilizes the language of the black melancholic turned narcissist as he gestures toward a black kingdom not on the long-since-forgotten continent but here, down the hill, in a place whose name speaks volumes about the American lack of subtlety, Clintonville. Moreover, this articulation of what looks surprisingly like Black American nationalism comes heavily freighted with concern over the complicated operations of gender and sexuality in the articulation of racial identity.

Tyree sits beside his son, who is Fish. He bequeaths his black kingdom to a son whose journey to manhood has been marked not only by the promiscuity of father and the steadfastness of mother but also by lynching, threat of castration, and thinly veiled sexual antagonism, cum attraction, between white men and black boys. As Tyree cranks the engine to the car and heads down the hill to one of his houses of prostitution so that Fish might have all the fun he wants, one is left with the impression that this monstrous turn, this change of Rex into Fish is a willed, indeed chosen, compromise with the racialist discourses by which "America" is structured. We see quite clearly the repression and subsequent mourning of what one might call a more generous version of male heterosexuality. That is to say, a king who is obliged to look one way but not the other is inevitably a somewhat funny fellow.

The protest that I imagine now from my readers rings so loudly in the hot silence of this now overly bright apartment that I think it best to get it out. I have admitted already to the privileging of biography in these pages. It is also quite easy for me to admit that this work is designed to valorize Wright, to resecure his status as "The Father of Contemporary Black American Literature," a phrase that I have used more or less lightly but that is invested with great meaning by even and especially Wright's most serious critics. I can also see at least the most obvious ways in which my work looks rather nostalgic. I have not, in fact, relinquished the gendered narratives of literary influence that I critique in this work. Instead I have borrowed these ungainly tools and put them to somewhat more ambitious, if rather predictable, purposes. Not only is Richard Wright understood here as The Father of Black American Literature, but to the extent that this literature operates as a primary node of the American cultural enterprise, one might easily nominate Wright as the progenitor, or at least *a* progenitor, of the variety of new developments in literature and the study of literature that establish the complexity of what I will call, with a bit of winking, the American canon. Sherley Anne Williams states the matter with passion and precision when she informs us that Wright

> also fathered a bastard line, racist misogyny—the denigration of black women as a justification for glorifying the symbolic white woman—and male narcissism—the assumption that racism is a crime against a black

man's sexual expression rather than an economic, political, and psychological crime against black people—that was to flower in the fiction of black writers of the late sixties and early seventies.[13]

Perhaps I have played my hand a bit too quickly here. For I mean to ask where it is that enterprises such as queer theory and feminism are settled within that territory that encompasses both Wright's legitimate progeny, "Negro Novelists and Third World Peoples," and his bastards, racist misogyny and the denigration of black women. I would also seriously question Williams's severely chalked line between sexuality and what she describes as "economic, political, and psychological crime." Still, my concern remains not only with the deployment of a rhetoric of fatherhood and reproduction in relation to Wright but also with the fact that this rhetoric enables Wright's status as (funny) public intellectual. Indeed what seems funniest about Wright's intellectualism is that his techniques for the production and maintenance of both celebrity and longevity are, in fact, infinitely reproducible. Or perhaps I am simply stating from another vantage point my earlier observation that Wright understood and desired that this moment, the moment of the presumably "queer" reading of "personal" evidence left by a "public" intellectual, would indeed come. If Wright is the promiscuous father that I suspect he is, then it is precisely this promiscuity that he has left to his varied and multihued progeny.

The question still to be answered concerns of course what may look like nostalgia for patrilineal narratives of influence. Great father. Less than grate-*ful* children. In answering this charge, it may be simpler and more honest just to plead guilty. As I said earlier, I fear my methods risk seeming out-of-date, perhaps even antique. In my own defense I would state again that my interest in Wright turns on that funniness that I have suggested mediates contemporary black intellectualism, a funniness that has as one of its constituent elements a certain well-maintained, childlike precocity turned intellectual promiscuity. One imagines entire clans of intellectuals checking their chronicles to find the family name, Wright, indiscreetly tucked between poets and politicians, celebrities and those universally celebrated for their lack of celebrity.

I return late then, if still a bit blushing, to the name of the father because I understand this naming as obviously and necessarily undone. It is this perennial lack of fixity, this promiscuity that allows for a great many of our current aesthetic, theoretical, and political practices. Thus I prefer to think of queer theory and feminism not so much as Wright's bastards as those unfortunate half castes produced, like *The Long Dream* itself, out of his earlier struggles with that white woman. Moreover, his legacy to them is hopefully more than a simple return of those no longer functional aspects of patriarchy all too often dumped on American intellectuals in the guise of tradition, discipline, and rigor but instead a particular talent for recognizing one's own implication in our varied and various practices of naming. One might learn from Wright not only the ways entry into public life is overdetermined by the particular name that one carries but also that there are some clever tricks to ameliorate the effects of that naming. The trick of the funny father, the gift that Wright willed us, is that his name is so versatile, so widely available that one might rightly make a claim upon it from any number of subject positions. Moreover, one of the clearest lessons Wright has for us is that the survivor, that character with the luck, not only knows his name, the standard narrative of his reproduction, but has an uncanny ability to name the naming process itself.

Wright expends incredible energy in *The Long Dream* explicating the manner in which early in his life Rex is reconfigured as Fishbelly or Fish. The man's name attached to a boy child was thrown by the wayside in an Oedipal ritual in which Rex's father, Tyree, brings home a batch of fish and his mother, Emma, proceeds to kill and gut them. Rex feels at once attracted to and threatened by the animals that his parents sacrifice. He is particularly bothered by the fact that the smell of the fish reminds him of the smell of his mother's body. The translation from Rex to Fish is not quite so easy, however, as a simple move from man to woman or perhaps heterosexual to homosexual. Wright is very careful, in fact, to make it clear that the challenge for the not quite modern black, living in a not quite modern America, is not so much that he possesses an unknown identity as the fact that one knows already that this identity is built upon a set of compromised desires, thwarted pleasures. When one places black and American side by side one immediately announces a subject who has been touched, handled, worked upon. The Black American, produced in the hothouse environment of Mississippi, becomes a sort of badly tended and too brutally grafted Bonsai whose final outcome can never be certain. He is always a mistake, no matter how beautiful he may become. Fish's name thus always carries the sense of being a bad, poorly understood joke. His father grabs a pile of fish bladders from the cutting board, puts one to his lips, and blows, creating a balloon of flesh. Rex is delighted by the "fish bellies" that his father produces and will not hear that they are actually fish bladders. His obstinacy becomes a bone of contention between him and his friends, and thus they begin to ridicule him with the child's name, Fish.

One is alerted from the outset, therefore, that the focus of *The Long Dream* is on the rather faulty narratives of reproduction available to American intellectuals. Or more precisely, we are reminded that there is something significant to be gained by remaining tuned to the alternative narratives available at those obscured, funny locations where the father's name fails to reproduce itself. Writing in the wake of a generation of feminists who themselves have picked up the rather finely stitched mantles thrown down by Lacan, I am tempted of course to utilize the language of the fold, that turning of the division between nature and culture back in upon itself that is marked most spectacularly by the name *mother*. One sees easily how Rex folds into Fish, how normative conceptions of masculinity are subsumed by one of the common names we give to our anxiety surrounding the mother and the unmentionable. Indeed this ritual in which Rex becomes Fish (the phrase is so ripe as to make comment unseemly) parallels our anxieties surrounding the ways in which it appears that mother, with her strange and compelling smell, stands outside of culture while simultaneously acting as the primary vehicle of our entry into culture. Wright anxiously plays here with the veil separating the putative law of the father from the mother's ability to operate within, through, and beyond that law by bending to it, by reestablishing the very norms of culture and society to which she herself is compelled to submit.

> "Don't you want to see the fishes papa brought?"
> Oh, she was holding a fish! With parted lips, he advanced and stared at the wriggling, gray shape. But *that* couldn't be a fish . . .
> "He little," he said.
> "He's big enough," she said.
> "He's alive?"
> "Yeah. But he won't be for long. I'm going to kill 'im."
> "How, Mama?"
> "I cut 'im open with a knife. You'll see." (Wright, 11)

What most startles one about Wright's aesthetic is not so much the fact of his relentless pursuit of answers to the most difficult theoretical riddles (Which gender is the black man really?) but instead his inability to turn away from the fold, away from the variety of narratives that presumably operate in the reproduction of the father's name. Papa exists here of course but *only* as a name. Indeed the father's name—like the father himself—is a rather promiscuous creature. One might easily misread this passage or read it with the precision of a child to understand the mother's question not as "Do you want to see the fish brought by papa?" but instead "Do you wish to have 'the fish father' brought?" In either case the instruction is both in the science of (re)articulating law and tradition as well as the complex art of understanding those many exceptions to "the law" that give both individual and law the flexibility, the stretch, necessary if one is to have any success at reproducing either tradition, laws *or* individuals.

Thus we would be well advised to pay attention not only to the obvious repressions in this text (Rex's father buys and sells women just as readily as he buys and sells fish) but also to what I will call the obvious become the insistent. Indeed what overwhelms this passage is not just fish but mother. Rex protests that the fish is small. His mother counters that he is big enough. He continues by pointing out that the fish is alive, but mother assures us that she will kill him soon enough. The double entendres here are patently simple to understand. Though Wright in no way suggests Emma, Rex's mother, is an equal player, much less a dominant one, in the games of cultural reproduction to which he introduces us, he does not allow us to forget that she does give life to Fish even as she takes it from fish. With knife in hand she engages in a sort of acrobatics of negation that work to so exaggerate the traditional prerogatives of the nurturer and giver of life as to make obvious the ways in which a variety of discourses are repressed, if certainly not destroyed, in the enactment of that very tradition.

It might seem at this juncture that we have strayed dangerously far from the basic concerns of this chapter, forgotten our earlier emphasis on the ways in which conceptions of black masculinity operate in the production of modern forms of public intellectualism. Indeed my interest in a half-realized fatherhood has morphed into a fascination with some odd species of overdetermined mothering. Indeed, as Hortense Spillers reminds us, the legacy slavery left to us all is a history of putative motherhood set against nonexistent fatherhood. Thus our ongoing efforts to establish—and reestablish—a modern narrative of black fatherhood, efforts of which Wright was a chief architect, are themselves dependent upon the deployment of a more familiar, if not necessarily more potent, narrative of black motherhood. Spillers writes,

The African-American male has been touched . . . by the mother, *handed by* her in ways that he cannot escape, and in ways that the white American male is allowed to temporize by a fatherly reprieve. This human and historic development—the text that has been inscribed on the benighted heart of the continent—takes us to the center of an inexorable difference in the depths of American women's community: the African-American woman, the mother, the daughter, becomes historically the powerful and shadowy evocation of a cultural synthesis long evaporated —the law of the mother—only and precisely because legal enslavement removed the African-American male not so much from sight as from *mimetic* view as a partner in the prevailing social fiction of the father's name, the father's law.[14]

I have suggested in this chapter that one of the major elements of what I have described as Wright's funniness has been his ability to articulate, and thus to mediate, intellectual celebrity from the vantage point of the child. My arguments would be impossible, moreover, if not for those many critics who have pointed to Wright's own rough handling of female characters in both his novels and autobiographies, critics who have consistently narrated Wright's presumed misogyny as evidence of unresolved tension between (Wright's) mother and her son. Still, when Spillers speaks of the African American male's having been *handed* by the mother, what she effects is more than a simple rearticulation of the anxiety surrounding so-called black matriarchy. Instead she suggests that black subjectivity comes into being at the very site at which the father's name is repressed. Thus black identity is not produced in private, in those domestic spaces containing the father's wealth, but in public, that location at which the child is handed, announced, named within society. Of course, I understand that embedded within Spillers's analysis is the history of the slave's forced removal, the separation of mother from child. I also recognize that there are many varieties of privacy available to black persons even as I maintain that blackness itself is always a public iteration. The choice that the mother makes at the moment of handing, however, is one that is predicated upon the necessity of the child's articulation of public identity, especially if that child's identity seems foreclosed already by the disciplines of private property. Again, therefore, funniness marks the spot at which choice and tradition are negotiated, that place at which intellectual and community establish and act upon their inevitable conflict.

Thus, though one finds within both weak and strong versions of Black American (cultural) nationalism notions of a Black American community and identity that remain veiled from the less than careful white interloper, it is nonetheless true that every articulation of "The Black American" reminds us of rather desperate concessions that we, the putative blacks, have allowed and endured within state and society. The name "Black" is, in fact, one of the most basic of American compromises. That is to say, the slave's rearticulation as "the black" places even more distance between the individual and his owner/lover/father's name. Thus "black" and its many unlikely cousins —colored, Negro, African—turn the linguistic and historical tables, as it were, filling a space that both precedes and follows slavery. It expresses nostalgia and melancholy while also evincing a profound engagement with not so much an imagined community as an imagined future.

We have returned repeatedly to the belief that Black American identity does not and cannot precede or supersede the production of the United States itself. Or to fold my arguments even more securely into the rhetoric of *Once You Go Black,* racial identity does not precede (erotic) struggle between master and slave, or even the vicious confrontations between capital and labor. Race is one method, one of many, that we have at our disposal in our ongoing efforts to obscure the operation of communal and individual agency in the articulation of the society that we have, in fact, created ourselves. Thus we would be wise to take heed of Spillers's attempts to remind us of the funny taste that black can leave in the mouth—funny in the way that it alerts us to articulations of freedom and choice available to even the most profoundly restricted of subjects, that effervescence suggesting the law of the mother. At the same time it disallows innocent narratives of our ancestors' steadfast resistance. Indeed the question remains, "Did our mothers actually *hand* us?" Does going black always involve turning back, imply the building of memorials to (black) nobility upon the repression of our unsettling knowledge of black agency, culpability, and compromise?

III

Fishbelly turned and saw plump, short, black Aggie West, a glove under his arm, coming mincingly toward him. Fishbelly frowned. West showed a wide, sweet smile.

"Hello, Rex," Aggie greeted Fishbelly by his Christian name.

Fishbelly scowled, for he despised anyone so pretentious as not to call him Fish. . . .

"Look, sissy! Beat it!" Zeke was harsh.

"I want to play ball," Aggie mumbled musically.

"Naw, you pansy," Fishbelly said. "Now, go!!"

"Why can't I play?" Aggie seemed indifferent to his frigid reception.

"Cause we don't want to play with fruits!" Sam snarled.

"Why don't you want to play with me?" Aggie enunciated correctly.

"Play the piano, you fairy," Tony said. "That's all you fit for!"

"I love to play the piano and I also love to play ball," Aggie explained.

"Homo, leave us alone!" Fishbelly's eyes were like brown granite.

—Wright, *The Long Dream*

There are many awkward moments in *The Long Dream,* many sentences populated by unlikely characters carrying seemingly extraneous elements into an already heavily burdened plot. And the several appearances of Aggie West certainly rank high among these. Thus Aggie's entry onto the field of play does not represent so much the return of the repressed as one of the more articulate moments in the naming of the process of repression itself. The boys stumble over their insults, not knowing whether to frame Aggie as sissy, pansy, fruit, fairy, or homo. Aggie, whose name suggests home, land, and wholesome community, is one of the several characters whom Wright allows to represent what I have called Black American civility. Aggie concedes readily to the name given to Fishbelly presumably by both father and mother, Rex. This while Aggie's own genealogy includes the name of no father (or perhaps it contains the names of too many). Thus Aggie might rightly (or Wrightly) be called simply, Black. He is then most certainly funny, but funny only to the extent that he represents that tear, that remarkable fold where the black comes into being. The boys tease him and indeed throw stones, opening an ugly wound on the back of his head, from which "a sheet of blood gushed, flooding the back of Aggie's shirt, forming a red collar about his neck" (39). In the process, however, they *graphically* reveal a fear that one might choose to narrate as simple homophobia but that also turns on the difficulties faced by the careful, or perhaps I should say honest, student of American culture when he or she attempts to distinguish the perversity of the homosexual from the unacceptability of the black.

This first scene of Aggie's comes quick on the heels of one in which Fishbelly himself has been accosted by a group of white gamblers who believe that roughly handling a young black boy will bring luck, a word that "sounded bad" to Fish, that "rhymed with a word that he had heard a boy say at school and the teacher had washed out the boy's mouth with soap" (15). Again Wright studs the scene with the most obvious signals of sexual profligacy. "'When a nigger cries, that's proof he's got luck,' the man holding him said. 'Them tears of his is like virgin's blood. His luck ain't never been touched. Roll them dice, nigger'" (15–16). While some might chafe at the notion that the assault here is sexual, I believe that there can be no hesitation in our understanding of the fact that what is stolen from Fish is, in fact, virginity. Indeed if the black does possess uncanny luck, then it is undoubtedly tied up with the manner in which black identity "jes grew," to borrow one of Stowe's clumsier constructions. While the articulation of blackness implies the disarticulation of the name of the father, it also implies the opening up of new possibilities in our efforts to name and reproduce subjectivity. Indeed when we say "black" we conjure the very luck that presumably one encounters at the edge of frontier. Black marks the spot at which the names of individuals become impossibly intertwined with those given homes and communities.

Thus Aggie West's own impossibly overdetermined name might itself mark the site of a sort of funny fatherhood. Aggie West is a child's name that resonates rather tellingly with Clintonville. Where the one begins and the other ends is difficult to say. "Move on, queer nigger!" Zeke screamed. Shove off!" As the blood pours in sheets down the back of Aggie's head we are returned to that image of a black giant, trussed up like Gulliver, given to us by Ralph Ellison. For if the black, the nigger, represents America's metaphor, the game of racial naming that we cannot seem to do without, then one might ask with all seriousness how much more queer could a queer nigger be? It seems appropriate then that I reiterate my earlier comments concerning the distinction between queer and funny. That is to say, Aggie's funniness might still be explained as the awkwardness of a child, thus allowing one, at least in theory, to leave off full consideration of his sexuality. Indeed the pleasure that one senses Wright took in writing this scene turned on his ability to play again on the ground of children, to wade into the mass of erotic tension existing under the sign "Clintonville" but to do so among a constituency who if not exempted from sexual activity are certainly trained to postpone announcing themselves as sexual beings within the greater confines of their society.

Even more important, however, is the fact that Aggie, like Wright, has the ability not simply to acknowledge the contradictions inherent in the lived experience of America but also the temerity to make use of those contradictions, to access those folds and tears, in order to manipulate, with varying degrees of success, entry into public discourse. I argue, therefore, that it is precisely this funny aspect of Aggie's character that most alerts us to his genealogy, makes one consider again Baldwin's tortured reading of Wright and Stowe's thrusting and counterthrusting. I do not mean to imply that the so-called funny black is a character who straightforwardly "resists" the processes of naming with which we have been concerned. Indeed within the logic of this chapter, Aggie carries the mark of both Wright and Stowe. And if he lacks grace as he struggles beneath this considerable weight, then he more than makes up for it with resolve. Aggie is a character who recognizes that names represent choices, not destinies—again a small distinction but one that seems to make all the difference, or at least the difference that matters, as plump, short, black Aggie, a child literally overburdened with names (none of which exactly spells father), enters the emerging social world that *The Long Dream* represents. It is not just that Aggie is indifferent to the insults that are thrown at him. Instead Wright is extremely clever in his pairing of the "passive resistance" that would soon become so celebrated a strategy in American political life with the queerness that this passivity implied. Aggie looks surprisingly similar then to any number of black "supplicants" who have come before America's many kings to make their humble requests.

In offering these arguments, I am strongly supported by the militant rigor with which Wright reiterates "the queer's" ability to model the difficulties faced by "the nigger" in the social and discursive worlds that he makes available in *The Long Dream*. The boys remark after attacking Aggie that "we treat 'im like the white folks treat us." And strangely enough it seems true that the wound that they inflict upon the fat, black body of their countryman, their homeboy, anticipates the several literally gaping wounds that will be inflicted upon the black body of Clintonville. The tear in the back of Aggie's head, that sheet of blood forming in a ring about his neck, prepares us for the homoerotic rage on display in the lynching of Chris, a boy who had earlier taught Fish about baseball and condoms but who, caught in the hotel room of a white prostitute, had had his genitals removed with a pair of pliers, so that as Fish looks at the corpse laid out on one of his father's examination tables, he fixates on the "coagulated blot in a gaping hole between the thighs and, with defensive reflex, [lowers] his hands nervously to his groin (77).

Moreover, it is Aggie who reminds us with his telltale use of Fish's *Christian* name of the easy manner in which Fish might himself have been substituted for Chris. Aggie's greatest crime, however, the insult for which he is beaten and harassed but not quite silenced, is that he refuses to disavow the lessons learned at the knee of mother, the reality that even and especially the most vicious names hurled against the black subject carry with them the hint of melancholy, the longing for love, kin, property, that yearning marked by the name Black. "You have to be terribly attracted toward a person, almost in love with 'im, to mangle 'im in this manner," Tyree's business partner, Dr. Bruce, announces glibly as he performs a sort of affective and discursive postmortem. "They hate us . . . but they love us too; in a perverted sort of way, they love us—"

One might well predict at this juncture that I will attempt to recalibrate traditional Freudian narratives of triangulation in order to reestablish the subjectivity and agency of that anomalous figure, the queer black, the subject who is violently hated and even more violently loved. And certainly I do think that Aggie West's entry into the annals of American literary history ought to be celebrated. I am not yet ready, however, to remark him finally as queer. The labels "homo" and "queer nigger" are never chosen within this narrative but instead are thrown at Aggie precisely as a critique of the pretense—and audaciousness—evident in his name and character. I already have nominated Aggie as funny, but of course in doing so I mean only to suggest that his status as a child disallows his easy assimilation into the queer, thus the difficulty the boys have in establishing a proper name for him. It seems time then that I state the obvious, allow myself to make the bolder, more insistent claim that bubbles beneath the surface of this narrative. What seems patently apparent at this juncture is that it is precisely this funny subject position, this not quite radical but nonetheless militantly practical orientation toward one's environment, that Wright himself attempted to inhabit in his efforts to be understood as that strangest of anomalies, the articulate subaltern.

Aggie's text—"Hello, Rex," "I want to play ball," "Why can't I play?" "Why don't you want to play with me?" "I love to play the piano and I also love to play ball"—cleverly folds the erotic, the political, and the aesthetic into one loaded chain of reference. Indeed Aggie does not simply introduce the sexual with the phrase "play ball"; he also demonstrates the ways in which our most cherished intellectual and political projects are themselves overwritten by erotic narratives that it seems impossible to suppress. Of course what shocks us in a phrase as simple as "I love to play piano and I also love to play ball" is that Wright saw so clearly the awkwardness of the creative intellectual's attempts to represent himself as "just one of the boys." Playing the piano, still considered one of the chief arenas for the display of Black American folk genius, is here rendered as precisely that which divides intellectual from folk. (What then is one to make of the intellectual who writes novels, much less one who "reads" them?)

I would continue in this vein by suggesting that what *stuns*, what leaves one groggy and staggering, is Wright's daring to imply that even the most cherished narratives of American progress are structured by old-fashioned erotic tensions and yearnings. Aggie's entreaties unto Rex, his iteration of his desire, his constant questioning of the denial of that desire, as well as his articulation of his competence (indeed he does play ball *and* piano), suggests precisely the claims made upon American civil society by the Black American. With this observation I of course mean to alert my readers to those less than polite narratives of our recent history that treat our most distinguished leaders in the struggle for Black American civil rights as both "boys" who want to get into the game (whether their fingers have been trained to the discipline of the keyboard or not) as well as sissies, pansies, fruits, fairies, and homos who are attracted to the game's players, their power, their comradeship, and most especially their ability to exclude.

Now I believe I can set aside, at least for a moment, one of the major rhetorical strategies of this chapter. That is to say, though I have insisted on young Aggie's funniness, I am willing to concede at this juncture that he does indeed "develop" into a "queer adult." A second, "queer" narrative of Aggie becomes generally accepted in Clintonville, even as Aggie and especially his mother continually reiterate Aggie's funniness. "Mr. Tucker, please help me with Aggie," Aggie's mother begs an adult Fish.

> "He needs a job and nobody'll hire him. Why? I don't know. And he's a *good* boy; he sews, cooks, washes, irons, and takes care of the house. I ain't had a minute's trouble with 'im since he was born. He's polite, tidy, and bright as a button. But nobody'll give 'im any work. Now, is that fair, Mr. Tucker?"
>
> "What can Aggie do, Mrs. West?" Fishbelly had asked her once.
>
> "Just about *anything*," she said fervently.
>
> And Fishbelly had known that "anything" meant that Aggie could only play the piano. (196)

The evidence here is of course that in Clintonville and the America that Wright takes it to represent, the young man is not allowed the indulgences of the child. A black male who sews, cooks, washes, irons, takes care of the house, and plays the piano for good measure treads too heavily over the line separating the normatively masculine from the putatively feminine. Thus what Aggie's mother does not know is what the rest of the town already sees quite clearly, what Tyree Tucker himself announces without pause when Fish broaches the topic of hiring Aggie at the funeral home. "What would folks think if we had a 'fruit' working around them stiffs?" Tyree explodes. "Men wouldn't want to come to us to be buried even when they was *dead*," he continues cryptically.

> I once had a nineteen-year-old gal to fix up. Died of a bad heart. Her ma swore she was a virgin and mebbe she was. I don't know. But you know that gal's ma wouldn't leave my 'shop' till we buried that gal? Said her gal was a virgin and she wanted to make sure she was *buried* a virgin. (196–197)

Aggie becomes then that subject who stands in for all those many repressions of the discourses of sexuality, if not the varied practices of sex, upon which Clintonville is built. Indeed Tyree's fear is precisely that Aggie will be the spark that turns the obvious insistent, the queer element that makes the presence of the devoted mother brooding over the dead virgin body of her daughter seem not only appropriate but imperative. Indeed Aggie, if examined in the muted light of the funeral home, might begin to look too much like Fish, who for his part had only a short while before choked down a paper advertisement that he carried with him featuring a white woman clad only in her underwear. He did so while in the custody of the police in order to preempt even the assumption of what we might think of as heteronormativity.[15]

Fish's act of repression here has the effect of resituating the "female" object of desire from the outside in. He becomes delicate, fainting when he is threatened with castration by the policemen. And lest one squander the opportunity to recognize the ways in which discourses of blackness are overdetermined by discourses of queer sexuality, Wright puts the damning words directly in the mouths of Fish's assailants. Clem, who takes the lead in this ritual abuse, refers to Fish as "that cute-looking nigger with the big eyes." He then jokes, "Goddamn, ain't you got pretty hair, nigger. What you put in it?

Ham fat?" The joke is obvious but no less damaging for that. In a world in which any black ought to be flattered by the compliments of any white, but in which the opposite is almost never true, it is the simplest of maneuvers to point to the black's status as queer. Moreover, as I have reiterated throughout *Once You Go Black,* the shame (if we are indeed still concerned with such matters) of the Black American is not that he has kept quiet during such encounters but that sometimes he has put those big eyes and that pretty hair to good use, without of course the ham fat.

I would like to hold on, however, to the tension that makes itself apparent when we compare this "knowledge" of Aggie's queerness with that funny alternative knowledge offered by his mother. I would suggest in fact that my conceding Aggie's "queerness" ought not to preclude our serious consideration of his mother's narration of his funniness. For though doubt rests uneasily on this woman's words, we nonetheless find again that Wright credits her with uncanny prescience. In a world in which profound longing is relieved only by radical violence—the very violence enacted during Chris's lynching, mimed during Fish's two incarcerations, and militantly repeated with Tyree's murder and the unthinkable fire and grisly deaths at the Grove, the dance club where Fish's girlfriend worked as a prostitute—in such a world perhaps the only thing that one can do, the only thing that can be done, is to assert, even and especially in the face of the ridiculous, one's freedom, one's ability to choose, to name, to rename, to translate. That is to say, though one might live in a funny world in which desire is brutally hedged between tradition and choice, one still continues to maintain one's freedom, a freedom on which one must inevitably act.

I will turn in these final comments to two texts embedded within the fabric of *The Long Dream* that I believe speak to each other and us about this matter of the Funny Father's Luck, this ability of even the oppressed subject to voice his agency at precisely those moments when his very existence and that of his community are threatened. The first appears during the funeral for Tyree and those forty-two persons who died in the fire at the Grove. Again Fish and his doppelganger, Aggie, are at center stage. Indeed it seems that Aggie will have the last word as he takes his place, prominent in the pulpit, every step carefully mangled in Wright's exquisite narration so that Aggie West, the promise, is rearticulated as a mincing, too careful church organist with wet lips, body bent forward, and voice proceeding with unblushing melancholy.

Sunset and evening star
     And one clear call for me!
And may there be no moaning of the bar
     When I put out to sea.
But such a tide as moving seems asleep,
     Too full for sound and foam,
When that which drew forth out the boundless deep
     Turns again home. . . .
Twilight and evening bell,
     And after that dark!
And may there be no sadness of farewell
     When I embark;
For though from out our bourne of time and place
     The flood may bear me far,
I hope to see the Pilot face to face
     When I have crossed the bar. . . .
One sweetly solemn thought
     Comes to me o'er and o'er:
I'm nearer my home today
     Than I have ever been before . . .
(Wright, 320–321)

Though it is obvious that Aggie mourns here, it is also just as obvious that he yearns and celebrates that yearning. Indeed the image of sailing that Wright deploys suggests the departure from one home while promising a "return" to another unknown home, one in which the pilot and sailor come face-to-face, producing an affectional dyad that comes closer to simulating a named, if not properly established, "home" than ever before. At moments of departure then, at those many locations at which the known home is suddenly and viciously torn asunder, the only act left for the melancholic subject, the only choice, is precisely to figure a new home, to offer an alternative that falls somewhere between the will of the slaver and the affect of the mother. Indeed the luck that makes itself evident at such moments is the uncanny ability to name these ruptures, those tears, the itchy tinglings left on the palms of hands that once supported the weight of a child.

I will close with a brief discussion of the final scene in *The Long Dream*. It comes after much tragedy, after Chris's lynching, after Tyree's murder at the hands of his one-time associate, police chief Cantley, after the fire at the Grove, after Fish has been arrested for a second time in order to quell Cantley's concern that Fish possesses the canceled checks that prove that Tyree paid Cantley and that the two had a relationship that was not only collegial but also somehow familial. This scene, like the funeral, is extravagantly staged, coming as it does aboard an integrated airplane bound for Paris. Fish has finally arranged himself, like his nemesis, Aggie, within one of those many interstitial spaces available within and without (American) society. He is neither here nor there. Indeed it is only now, in this "location" dominated by the brooding femininity of the fifties flight attendant, that Fish is able to reflect, to write. Only here does he allow himself to draft a note to Mr. McWilliams, presumably the only honest white man in Clintonville, the stand-in for those many "honest" readers in liberal America. Therein, he attempts to comment upon what he has seen and experienced, to narrate, however awkwardly and haltingly, the truth of his own life.

> Dear Mr. McWilliams:
> I don't know what you are going to say or think of me when you get this letter and the canceled checks. I lied to you about these checks. Papa left them and I was just too scared to give them to you. You are going to say that I did not trust you and that I lied to you and you are going to be right. I did tell you a lot of lies. . . . Mr. Cantley could have killed me, but I wasn't going to say one word. I knew where the checks was hid all the two years I was in jail, but I knew that if I gave them to you Mr. Cantley would know who gave them and he would have had his men kill me just like he had his men kill Papa . . . I don't care no more. I don't know how long I'm going to be in France and don't ever mean to come back to Clintonville, Miss., to live any more. . . . Mr. McWilliams you are the only honest white man I ever met. You are more honest than I am. I was not honest with you cause I was scared, so don't think too hard of me for all the lies I told. I don't know what kind of work I'm going to do, but I'm not ever going to collect any more fees. I'm through with that kind of stuff. It killed my papa and it almost killed me. . . .
>
> Yours sincerely,
> REX (FISH) TUCKER (381–382)

One might of course read this note as a minor element, a contrivance. And indeed it does work ultimately to draw together the many frayed threads of Wright's exceptionally complicated narrative. At the same time, however, it returns us to the very questions with which we began this chapter. Wright's bold move here is not just that he precisely calibrates the moment of articulate narration with a moment of departure but also that he makes it clear that his own much-lamented departure from the United States is the absent referent. Fish, like Wright, is only able to make sense of Mississippi when he leaves Mississippi. What intrigues me in these final moments, however, what still leaves me sputtering, if not exactly speechless, is the manner in which Fish signs this letter. Indeed this revision of the father's name written in bold script and supported by an unlikely pair of diacritical marks, REX (FISH) TUCKER, suggests finally a newly established modern subject who means to inhabit precisely the funny subject position that I have ascribed to Wright, Aggie, and Fish. For while the putative name of the father, "Rex Tucker," is evident, "Fish" remains prominent, reminding one as ever of the smell of mother. Indeed these appellations have been subsumed within a newly chosen, formal name, the name taken at the moment of departure, the moment of handing, that seeks to deny neither past nor future, mother nor father. Fish possesses, he owns, the funny father's luck. He picks up the detritus of his society—"Rex," "Fish," "Tucker"—and fashions from it nothing less than a chosen and indeed free subjectivity. Funny, isn't it?

2

Ralph Ellison's Blues

> There is a Negro church, a Negro press, a Negro social world, a Negro sporting world, a Negro business world, a Negro school system, Negro professions; in short, a Negro way of life in America. The Negro people did not ask for this, and deep down, though they express themselves through their institutions and adhere to this special way of life, they do not want it now. This special existence was forced upon them from without by lynch ropes, bayonet and mob rule. They accepted these negative conditions with the inevitability of a tree which must live or perish in whatever soil it finds itself.
>
> —Richard Wright, "Blueprint for Negro Writing"

> There is a bit of the phony built into every American.
>
> —Ralph Ellison, *Going to the Territory*

We have been continually reminded ever since that remarkable day in 1952 when Ralph Waldo Ellison first exploded onto the American literary scene that the genius which took hold of Ellison and made itself known through his writing was indistinct from the genius on display in the performances of the greatest of twentieth-century blues and jazz musicians. Indeed even at the beginning of the twenty-first century this idea of a black music-inflected modernist aesthetic embedded within Ellison's work continues to function as a sort of pristine literary orthodoxy. And as Ellison himself celebrated his own early training as a trumpeter and often suggested that blues and jazz represented the apotheosis of Black American artistry, it is easy to understand why this idea has been left unchallenged. I will not be so rash then as to refute the contentions of either Ellison or his many students. Ellison was a man of music, both literally and figuratively. He was born, as his biographer, Lawrence Jackson, notes, at precisely that moment in American history when blues performance had seemingly reached its zenith with the help of sensational impresarios such as Ma Rainey and Bessie Smith, while jazz had been unleashed onto the general American public from its traditional breeding grounds in the New Orleans French Quarter.[1]

It follows then that his life's work, the work exemplified by his greatest accomplishment, *Invisible Man,* was precisely to articulate the Black American experience of the sublime and the ridiculous through idioms developed in the high (literary) culture of nineteenth-century America. Like the jazz performer, he took traditional forms, infused them with the rhythms of black life, and then improvised his way out of the mess that he had created. In the process, he helped both to change the tenor of the Black American vernacular and to broaden the scope of the American novel. This, however, is where most analyses of Ellison's "blues aesthetic" stop. I would suggest, therefore, that one of the cheap tricks that has been played on Ellison is that like grainy recordings of Walter Page or rare footage of Cab Calloway, Ellison and his works have become national artifacts, the difficult stuff given to ambitious high-school seniors as they attempt to master their first ten-page essays. Still, there is another question that haunts the oeuvre of Ralph Ellison.

Literary and cultural critic Jerry Gafio Watts provides an invaluable service when he reminds us that the first concern of any intellectual, Ellison included, is self-reproduction. As Watts puts it, writers want to write; painters want to paint.[2] Thus the knotty issue with which every serious student of Ellison must wrestle is the simple fact of the master's inability to publish a second novel in his own lifetime. Though he was able to write the great *Invisible Man* in Harlem under the most difficult of circumstances, winning the National Book Award in the process, he was not able to repeat this performance, even as a distinguished fellow of the American Academy in Rome. Where I would suggest that those critics who still focus on the matter of how blues and jazz affected Ralph Ellison and his work have gone astray then is not in their will to bend the precepts of one discipline to meet the needs of another—that is to say, their mixing of apples and oranges—but instead in their failure to ask the simple question of how Ralph Ellison's aesthetic, Ralph Ellison's Blues, if you will, might have contributed to the spectacular display of what some would call writing block but I prefer to think of as publishing block, which dogged Ellison from 1952 until his death.

I will ask then that my readers allow me a bit of leeway as I commit what may seem like literary critical heresy. I am concerned in these pages not with the novel that Ralph Ellison did publish but instead with the one that he did not, indeed the one that many would suggest he never truly completed, though it sits here on my desk, prominent among a pile of unread manuscripts, doggedly alive and vital. I should rush to say that I am not nearly as convinced as some others seem to be that Ellison's refusal, a word I have chosen carefully, to finish and publish his second novel, was a factor of the work's simply never congealing or the author's having lost his nerve. Instead I would submit that Ellison's Achilles heel may well have been the very fact that he invested so heavily in the notion that the Black American intellectual had necessarily to reproduce the vernacular within even his most abstract works if these works were to have true purpose. I would go further and suggest that this idea of a simple relationship between the intellectual's efforts and the folk's traditions was coming to seem less and less tenable to Ellison, particularly as he approached his second novel. Thus the master's "inability" to publish the work had as much to do with the ways in which the text challenged the most sacrosanct tenets of his former aesthetic as with any supposed diminution of talent.

Juneteenth, the novel that should never have been published, the bastard that like the descendants of Thomas Jefferson survives to mock its progenitor, bears an uncanny similarity to its own protagonists. The novel seems, in fact, like one last less-than-tasteful joke on the reputation of Ralph Ellison, just as the character Bliss, a presumably white child raised by black Daddy Hickman to be a preacher and a leader of the people, slips the yoke, as it were, and becomes the race-baiting Senator Sunraider. Strikingly, Ellison has very little to say in this work about blues, jazz, or the aesthetic traditions that grew out of them. Indeed the musician's craft is always figured as a thing of the past. Daddy Hickman played a horn before Bliss came to him but put it down when a distraught white woman, the very woman who had caused his brother's lynching with a false cry of rape, placed a new-born baby-mouse-red Bliss into his lap, without even bothering to give him the name of the boy's father. Indeed her purpose in coming to Hickman, in entering the house of her enemy, her victim, is to make amends for the harm she has caused by intervening into the familiar genealogical narratives that so plague America and Americans. A white woman gives a black man a baby-mouse-red child to replace the black brother whom her ugly, desperate words have doomed. And Daddy can no longer play his horn.[3]

It would seem, therefore, that we are right to suggest that Ellison is concerned in *Juneteenth* (much of which was written presumably in a borrowed apartment in a pleasant neighborhood of Rome) with the matter of how the forced intimacy of black and white, these so-called natural adversaries, necessitates a break with one vein of tradition (Daddy can no longer play his horn) and the resuscitation of another (Daddy and the black/white child, Bliss, become preaching sensations). Ellison ventures dangerously close to that precipice that confounds even and especially the most engaged of engaged intellectuals. He asks how one might produce one's art while also maintaining allegiance to one's community and the right-minded political and social movements that this community produces. How does the committed intellectual reproduce himself? His answer is that the artist who self-consciously yokes himself to the cause of his people must do so not so much at the expense of his art as at the expense of any sense of transparency. Alonzo Hickman is a rambling, womanizing, hard-drinking jazz man, but he is honest. Daddy Hickman is a pious, abstinent, and community-minded minister, but he is patently dishonest. He carries Bliss in on his shoulders, bright and white, destined to lead his people forward out of the American purgatory of segregation. And miraculously yet another set of traditional genealogies attach themselves to the child. Black woman, white rapist, discarded baby; white woman, black lover, discarded baby; Daddy need not attempt a more sophisticated narrative of the fair little boy's life history. Mama's baby. Papa's maybe.

Of course what is being remarked here is the difference between innocence and sophistication, that thing which distinguishes the so-called organic intellectual living in seamless communion with his community from those cynically cosmopolitan characters, like Ellison, who understand just how much artifice and bluster underwrite even our most cherished traditions. It is in this sense that Ellison might be said to have most profoundly betrayed his own early aesthetic pronouncements. Indeed as many of my readers know already, Ellison was skeptical of those artists who sacrificed their art to the exigencies of politics or the cold logics of sociology. This is exactly the critique that Ellison, and more frequently his friend and "critical enforcer," Albert Murray, made repeatedly against Ellison's most significant rivals, Richard Wright and James Baldwin.

Speaking of Baldwin, Murray informs us that the "best-selling novel, *Another Country* . . . reflects very little of the rich, complex, and ambivalent sensibility of the novelist, very little indeed, no more than does the polemical essay, *The Fire Next Time*." Instead Murray argues that these works represent Baldwin's "involvement with oversimplified library and laboratory theories and conjectures about the negative effects of racial oppression." He reserves the full force of his vitriol, however, for that black literary apostate, Richard Wright:

living in Paris among the most famous French existentialists, who then were having a field day protesting against U.S. can goods, refrigerators, automobiles, and most of all U.S. dollars in the hands of U.S. citizens, Wright, who seemed to regard himself as, so to speak, U.S. Negro-in-residence, gave them additional U.S. absurdities and atrocities to protest about. . . . He was by way of becoming something of an existentialist himself, but he was still given to ripping red hot pages of accusations from his outraged and smoldering typewriter and angrily flinging them all the way back across the Atlantic and into the guilt ridden lap of America. During this time, he also flung one such book at the guilt ridden face of pagan Spain and two or three at the guilt ridden face of white folks everywhere.[4]

One cannot appreciate fully the vigor with which Murray offers his critique of James Baldwin and especially Richard Wright unless one understands that these two giants always operate as foils for the far less productive, if presumably far more talented, Ellison. Murray argues that it is Ellison and not Baldwin or Wright who truly makes something of the fact that "the most old-fashioned elements in the blues tradition are often avant garde by the artistic standards of most other countries in the world." He goes on to suggest that Ellison surpassed Wright in "Richard Wright's Blues," Ellison's treatment of Wright's autobiography, *Black Boy,* and, moreover, that *Invisible Man* was the best first novel to appear since *Buddenbrooks.*[5]

This is exactly the point, however, at which Murray, caustic and fire-spitting as he is, demonstrates the rather surprisingly soft underbelly of his argument. For though he favorably compares Ellison to Baldwin, Wright, Faulkner, Hemingway, Malraux, and even Mann, he necessarily draws attention to the fact that these writers continued to produce novels over long periods, thereby making themselves vulnerable to exactly the type of critique that Murray launches. Much of the hostility that he demonstrates toward Baldwin and Wright turns, in fact, on the indisputable reality of these men's productivity, those many red hot pages of accusation thrown into the guilt-ridden laps of white people everywhere.

Tellingly, Murray has particular disdain for both internationalism and what one might think of as literary scientism. Richard Wright is criticized as much for living in decadent France and writing about pagan Spain as he is for being a bad writer, one just as bad, Murray informs us, as Jean-Paul Sartre himself. Indeed the insult that Wright has thrown at the American public is not so much his detailing of absurdities and atrocities, something that neither Murray nor Ellison were above, but instead his abandonment of the cadences and peculiarities of Black American folk culture for the sterile insights offered by the "science" of existentialism.

I would caution you, however, not to assume that what we are witnessing is simply a sort of black high-culture turf fight, though I will admit that there is an abundance of critical cattiness on display. Still, the grievances expressed here run much deeper than one might imagine. Murray's testy reproaches stand at the very center of not only his aesthetic but also that of Ralph Ellison himself. Ellison reminds us in the very first pages of *Shadow and Act* that his practice as an artist involves "a ceaseless questioning of those formulas through which historians, politicians, sociologists, and an older generation of Negro leaders and writers—those of the so-called Negro Renaissance—had evolved to describe my group's identity, its predicament, its fate and its relation to the larger society and the culture which we share." He goes on to relate an incident that happened while he was a student at Tuskegee Institute, a story remarkable as much for the sharp focus into which it brings Ellison's understanding of art and culture as for its stark depiction of the banality of American racism.

> I had undergone, not too many months before taking the path which led to writing the humiliation of being taught in a class in sociology at a Negro college (from Park and Burgess, the leading textbook in the field) that Negroes represented the "lady of the races." This contention the Negro instructor passed blandly along to us without even bothering to wash his hands, much less his teeth.[6]

Ellison is fighting here, but the rules of engagement are not nearly as clear as they might at first appear. It would seem that his struggle is to stamp out the romantic racialism that has been so productive for American intellectuals. One imagines a young, precocious trumpeter distressed that on the campus of Tuskegee, still a great center of Black American influence in the 1930s, when Ellison was a student, that the focus of the instruction was not to prove the modernity of the Black American but, on the contrary, to always remark him as overly sensitive and lacking initiative, the veritable "lady of the races." The obstacle that one immediately confronts, however, the conceptual thicket that Ellison never fully escaped, is the fact that even though Burgess and especially Park were notorious racialists—and perhaps racists—they nonetheless were self-consciously involved in an effort to document, theorize, and bring into being Black American modernity.

One must wonder if the vitriol that Ellison unleashed against Park and that unnamed Negro instructor was not grounded, at least in part, in the tension that any serious thinker might experience when faced with the task of establishing intellectual novelty in relation to the strident demand that Black American writers represent, always and ever, the profundity of a static Black American tradition. I would suggest, in fact, that the incredible strength and creativity displayed by American sociologists at midcentury were the results of the continual return to this same tension by the most skilled and sensitive practitioners of the discipline.

Robert Park, the father of the Chicago School of sociology, began his career as the assistant to Tuskegee's founder, Booker T. Washington. He was, in fact, a pivotal player in the creation of the Tuskegee machine, the most significant Black American power center of the late nineteenth and early twentieth centuries. Further, he helped train a number of prominent black social scientists, including Oliver Cox, Horace Cayton, Charles Johnson, and the iconoclastic E. Franklin Frazier. More important still, Park played a central role in Booker T. Washington's articulation of the accommodationism that, as I argued in the introduction, was understood as a key tool in the ongoing efforts to establish a viable class of black artisans. Thus, for better or worse, the goal of Park and Washington was to produce and reproduce the modern black worker. One might supplement this with the knowledge that, as Carla Capetti and others remind us, Richard Wright himself owed a great deal of his materialist aesthetic to the efforts to document urban pathology that were a hallmark of "Chicago sociology."[7] Bigger Thomas is, therefore, a character who has a great deal in common with the many unnamed "characters" in Park's own studies. Moreover, if one concedes the idea that Bigger initiates the contemporary phase of Black American literature, then it follows that naturally one is likely to find traces of Bigger and thereby Park in Ellison's own finely wrought portraits. Park was, therefore, a figure with two faces, one turned toward the culture and traditions of the folk, Africans only recently become American, and the other fixed firmly on the future, a future in which tradition would be sacrificed to the necessity of speed, flexibility, transparency, and ingenuity.

I will suggest to you then that Ellison and Park are, in fact, traveling within exactly the same conceptual territory. Indeed the main differences between them are more matters of emphasis than of substance. Park's primitivism leads him to believe that the Negro brings only his sensitivity and constant good humor to the welcome table of American modernity. Ellison is certain that the Negro has a wealth of folk knowledge abetted by a tradition of survival that makes him quintessentially American, a natural patriot. Indeed the struggle between Ellison and Park looks from this distance remarkably similar to the struggle between Daddy Hickman and Bliss, Jim and Huck, or any number of black/white couples lost in the ever-expanding terrain of the American national consciousness. Thus Ellison is every bit as much a primitivist or, if you prefer, pastoralist as is Park. His critical writing is, in fact, liberally seasoned with evocations of black folk consciousness that have the ability to make one at least catch one's breath, if not gag outright.

Such is the case with Ellison's description of a southern cleaning woman whom he had hired to help his wife in their New York home. He assures us that both he and his wife liked the woman but nonetheless had to fire her because "she simply wouldn't do her work." He seeks solace from friend and ever-ready muse Albert Murray, who reminds him,

> "You know how we can be sometimes. . . . She saw the books and the furniture and paintings, so she knew you were some kind of white man. You couldn't possibly be a Negro. And so she figured she could get away with a little boondoggling on general principles, because she's probably been getting away with a lot of stuff with Northern whites. But what she didn't stop to notice was that you're a *Southern* white man."[8]

Among the many startling things about this passage is the fact that though Ellison expends so much energy emphasizing his western and frontier roots, he ultimately settles on this idea of himself as white southerner, a subject position that remains just as static as that of the recently transplanted black maid. Indeed origin seems to take precedence over all other concerns, so much so that presumably traditional southern values eclipse questions of race, class, location, or the simple fact that one of the "southerners" involved in this exchange actually comes from the West, and both meet not among lilacs and weeping willows but instead among skyscrapers and smokestacks.

Even as I argue this point, however, even as I stress the idea that Ellison, like Park, engages readily in a species of primitivism, that he understands there to be black, southern, and American subjectivities that are essentially unchanging and unchangeable ("You know how we can be"), I would also suggest that the stakes here are somewhat higher than a sophomoric desire to demonstrate bad form on the part of one of the most distinguished of twentieth-century Black American writers. Yes, it is true that Ellison and Park are "locked together in a deadly, timeless battle." Yes, it is true that they represent, as James Baldwin suggests of Richard Wright and Harriet Beecher Stowe, opposite sides of the same erotic coin.[9] Still, I would remind you that the question that animates this discussion concerns not so much what Ellison did say and publish but instead what he did not. Moreover, the answer lies, I believe, somewhere in that dark and difficult space, that frontier territory, at which "the lady of the races" transforms herself into the southern white man.

Of course my concern now is with the varieties of desire on display in these passages. Though it is infrequently noted, the presumed insult at the heart of Parks's claims is the idea that the Black American is necessarily receptive, ever waiting to be taken, filled, made whole and modern, or, if you will allow me to stretch this metaphor to its limits, "known." Park came to know the Negro so well, in fact, that when he left Tuskegee after seven years in the service of Booker T. Washington he felt confident enough to write his mentor that he believed himself to be "for all intents and purposes, for the time, a Negro."[10] This recognition of the Negro's remarkable openness, his infinite ability to be known and experienced, helps one understand better Ellison's response to his first introduction to Park. That is to say, after a violation one ought at the very least to wash the hands, if not the teeth.

It makes perfect sense then that Ellison's confrontation with Park should consist partially in the act of donning the mask of (southern) white masculinity. Indeed the joke that Ellison cracks here is almost perfect in form and execution. For not only does he usurp the very position of white master that Park so comfortably inhabits, but also by framing himself as a *southern* master he begs the question of the owner's prerogatives, sexual and otherwise, over the slave. This all brings us, strangely enough, back to Ellison's quarrel with Richard Wright, whose aesthetic, once supported by Ellison but later abandoned for a much more sympathetic conception of folk culture, allows the Negro no location for cultural self-determination. Church, press, social world, business world, school system, and the Negro professions all have been forced upon the Negro community by lynch rope, bayonet, and mob rule. I would argue, moreover, that for Ellison this idea of Negro culture as the ultimate result of white violence is indistinct from Park's theses regarding ladies and races.

In "Richard Wright's Blues," one finds Ellison already in struggle with Wright even as he applauds the anger and realism so evident in *Black Boy*. The work of the essay, in fact, is to convert the more-established author's hard-won materialism into a mode of hyperarticulate blues improvisation. Thus in what is perhaps Ellison's most famous line of criticism he informs us that Wright has "converted the American impulse toward self-annihilation and 'going under-ground' into a will to confront the world."[11] Wright, whose autobiography proved to be yet another astonishing success but who nonetheless was taken to task for writing such a stark and presumably unbalanced picture of Black American life, is here understood as engaging in the infinitely respectable folk practice of telling it like it is, of chewing on the bitter reality of American racism then spitting it out in the form of the blues man's soulful refrain.

The repressed element within this all-too-familiar narrative is of course Richard Wright himself, who was notoriously suspicious of all versions of folk culture. This explains why Ellison would later see fit to make a remarkably seamless about-face. Indeed he would come to understand that it was he himself and not Wright who most successfully expressed the aesthetic tradition that he tried to articulate in "Richard Wright's Blues."

> I felt that Wright was overcommitted to ideology—even though I, too, wanted many of the same things for our people. You might say that I was much less a social determinist. But I suppose that basically it comes down to a difference in our concepts of the individual. I, for instance, found it disturbing that Bigger Thomas had none of the finer qualities of Richard Wright, none of the gaiety. And I preferred Richard Wright to Bigger Thomas. Do you see? Which gets you in on the—directs you back to the difference between what Wright was himself and how he conceived of the individual; back to his conception of the quality of Negro humanity.[12]

One can see clearly Ellison's movement out of the role of literary apprentice to that of master novelist. The more mature Ellison understands himself as having trumped the work of Wright precisely by immersing himself within the folk culture that his erstwhile mentor held at bay. But still, Daddy Hickman cannot play his horn. And more damning still, Ellison cannot repeat his performance. He cannot yoke that great fount of Black American folk culture and consciousness in order to achieve that most impressive artistic accomplishment, longevity.

I

That was the end of the old life for me, though I didn't know it at the time. But what does a man ever know about what's happening to him? She came in there heavy and when she went out I had his weight on *my* hands. What on earth was I going to do with a baby? I wasn't done with rambling, the boys were waiting for me out in Dallas. I hadn't even met a woman I thought I'd want to marry, and later when I did she wouldn't have me because she insisted I had been laying around with a white gal because she thought I was traveling with a half-white baby. So not only had the woman placed a child on my hands, she made me a bachelor. And maybe after that night, after seeing what a woman could be, after that revelation of their boundless nerve and infinite will to turn a man's feelings into mush and rubber, I had lost the true will to join with one forever in matrimony. I was still young and full of strength but after that I could only come so close and no closer. I had been hit but I hadn't discovered how bad was the damage. Master, did you smile? Did you say, "Where's your pride now, young man?" Did you say, "*How now, Hickman, can you hear my lambs a-crying? You've got to do something, son; you can't stand on the air much longer. How now, Hickman?*"

—Ralph Ellison, *Juneteenth*

One of the more daunting moments for any critic, indeed one of the most frightening, is not that point at which he finds himself surprised by the obvious implications embedded within the work that he has undertaken but instead that instant at which he recognizes that whether he chooses to dwell upon the truths that stare up at him from the page or not, they are there for all to see. This is indeed the place at which the critical enterprise becomes dangerous, the moment at which the text that was previously a monstrous thing composed of notes, coffee, and the confused musings of sympathetic colleagues comes alive and takes on (dare I say it?) a blissful independence. It is my suspicion, moreover, that exactly the same is true for the novelist.

What can no longer be denied, then, what insists on being recognized, indeed what I am certain already has been recognized, is the complex manner in which the text that is now being written, *Once You Go Black,* and the text that presumably never was written, *Juneteenth,* are both structured through and by complex systems of desire and eroticism that neither author is capable of fully controlling. I have expended considerable energy demonstrating what I believe to be the obviously homoerotic exchange between Ralph Ellison and Robert Park, an exchange made more complex still when one takes into consideration the deep implication of Richard Wright, James Baldwin, Albert Murray, and even Ernest Hemingway in the Ellison oeuvre.[13] It is clear to me, moreover, that Leslie Fiedler's seminal essay (all puns intended), "Come Back to the Raft Ag'in, Huck Honey!" stood flat-footed and menacing in the back of Ellison's mind as he worked through the passages that would become *Juneteenth.*[14]

Fiedler's controversial gambit of centering not only "race relations" in his analyses of the production of American literature and culture but also the manner in which American racial concerns are undergirded by a (repressed) homoeroticism anticipated the sea change in critical theory brought about through the efforts of Eve Kosofsky Sedgwick and others some forty years later. By pointing to the simple fact that the rivalry between black and white Americans is both sexualized and homosocial, if not homoerotic, Fiedler touched a rather raw nerve in the American critical enterprise. He spoke to the obvious reality that even in our most rarified moments of theoretical engagement, Americans, including American critics, remain obsessed with what the other fellow has going on "down there."[15] Ellison himself had already breached this difficult topic in "Beating That Boy," arguing that "it is impossible for the white American to think of sex, of economics, his children or of sweeping socio-political changes, without summoning into consciousness fear-flecked images of black men."[16]

I wish, however, to push the envelope a bit, to press both Ellison and myself by noting that the game here is not as one-sided as it appears. Though I concur with Ellison's contention that "fear-flecked images of black men" stand at the center of what some clumsily label "white consciousness," it is also true that images of the white man, some might even say the white master, radically structure "black consciousness." I would add to this only that it is impossible to distinguish one set of concerns, the obsession of white with black, from the other, the equally strong obsession of black with white. Even as the nigger settles himself rather securely in the proverbial woodpile the white man pitches his rickety tent within rather embarrassingly intimate striking distance. All I mean to do here then is to suggest that much of what we label desire is nothing more than conditioned response to ideological structures that function only insofar as the fact of their artificiality, their phoniness, remains obscured.

As I have stated repeatedly, I have considerable appreciation for many of the arguments regarding morality and Black American subjectivity that Ellison advances in *Juneteenth*. I believe, however, that what we must now acknowledge is that these arguments are themselves overdetermined by a homoerotic subtext that it is no longer possible to ignore. Indeed what Ellison confronts in this novel is the simple fact that the most sacrosanct notions of desire might be easily, if unexpectedly, denatured within modern life and literature. That is to say, when a crazy white woman breaks into your house, gives birth to a baby, then leaves when the child starts to become attached, becomes too accustomed to the warmth and smell of breast and nipple, perhaps the only thing the modern black intellectual can do is pick the baby up and see to its upbringing. That moment, however, the moment at which one refuses to recognize the child of one's traditional enemy as itself an enemy is the very moment at which the Black American subject, or at least the Black American male subject, becomes denatured or, if you prefer, queer. To pick up the rhythms of Ellison's sermon, Daddy Hickman can no longer ramble, and yet he is a bachelor. He should be hard as the boys waiting in Dallas, but his feelings have been turned to mush and rubber. And like a woman, he hears the crying of the lambs no matter the color of their fleece. Daddy Hickman can no longer play his horn.

He can, however, play Bliss. He can and does use the image of the white Negro, the Negro cleansed of Ham's muddy stain, to create what for Ellison is ultimately, I believe, an artificial narrative of redemption. He can and does produce out of the miniature orchestra that Bliss provides an African American symphony, of sorts, an extended riff on the themes of capture, bondage, torture, and of course freedom and jubilation—exactly the type of thing evoked by the ritualized singing of spirituals at Tuskegee or even the more high-brow Fisk. He can articulate profound black tradition by using the very artificiality and cynicism against which that tradition presumably stands.

> "But where did we come from, Daddy Hickman?"
> "We come here out of Africa, son; out of Africa."
> "Africa? Way over across the ocean? The black land? Where the elephants and monkeys and the lions and the tigers are?"

"Yes, Rev. Bliss, the jungle land. Some of us have fair skins like you, but out of Africa too."

"Out of Africa truly, sir?"

"Out of the ravaged mama of the black man, son."

"Lord, thou hast taken us out of Africa . . ."

"Amen, out of our familiar darkness. Africa. They brought us here from all over Africa, Rev. Bliss. And some were the sons and daughters of heathen kings . . ."

"Some were kings, Daddy Hickman? Have we of the younger generation heard you correctly? Some were kin to kings? Real kings?"

"Amen! I'm told that some were the sons and daughters of kings . . ."

". . . Of kings! . . ."

"And some were the sons and daughters of warriors . . ."

". . . Of warriors . . ."

"Of fierce warriors. And some were the sons and daughters of farmers . . ."

"Of African farmers . . ."

". . . And some of musicians . . ."

". . . Musicians . . ." (Ellison, *Juneteenth*, 119)

The melody with which Ellison teases us should be remarkably familiar to any person with even the slightest knowledge of contemporary Black American culture. Writing during the middle 1950s and beyond, when there was essentially no living memory of slavery much less the continent of Africa itself, Ellison evokes the sense of vertigo that one often feels when witnessing the celebration of "traditional" West African customs in the parks of San Francisco or hearing the grand virtues of Ethiopian kings extolled in the streets of Cincinnati. Though the tune that Daddy Hickman plays is pleasant, even catchy, it seems somehow unfinished. The suggestion here is that like American popular music, the traditional narrative of Black American bondage and redemption is itself an attempt to avoid certain rather obvious truths. Where did we come from? Here. Who are my ancestors? Mother: crazy white woman. Father: unknown.

One imagines that it is possible to produce narrative out of what we know to be the reality of black and American existence. Indeed *Juneteenth* is itself one such attempt. The great difficulty, however, is that in creating a "realistic" story, in building a narrative based on our awareness that American history is clouded in half truths and blind alleys, we disallow the production of grand scenarios or what one might call crescendo. It is not so much, I would argue, that the black, white, yellow, brown, red peoples who created this nation all have skeletons in their respective ethnic closets but instead that our heroism is so very complicated. Pick up a baby-mouse-red infant who would die otherwise and one instantly becomes a traitor to the race, a traitor to the highest principles of manly self-regard. Tell that baby the truth of its existence and one risks creating a monster, a thing always turned against itself, the ugly hermit rejecting all intimacy. The alternative, Ellison seems to suggest, is to produce increasingly obscene variations on already worn-out themes. Thus for Ellison the true tragedy in American culture is that we see fit to skip the often less-than-wholesome story of our actual history as a nation, a history that, as Ellison reminds us, "happened body to body, belly to belly over the long years" (Ellison, *Juneteenth*, 162). In place of that truth, the obvious become the insistent; we substitute myths of origin, minstrels' tales of immaculate conception and birth.

Here then is where the true struggle between Daddy and Bliss takes place. For Daddy still has the desires of the rambling musician without the discipline of the committed composer. So though he cannot tell Bliss or the many congregations that he serves with Bliss the true story of the boy's birth, a story with no heroes, he creates from the mystery that surrounds their intertwined lives a compelling, bluesy narrative that helps to push the man/boy preacher act into the realm of backwoods, evangelical celebrity. " 'Come on out here, Bliss,' " Daddy Hickman said, " 'I got something to show you.' " And Bliss did walk with Daddy through the garden, past the grape ardor and into the coolness of the barn. And there he saw his fate. It sat atop a pair of saw horses and took the form of long narrow box.

> "What is it?" he asked. "It's for the service. For revivals . . ." Daddy answered. "It's for you to come up out of. You're going to be resurrected so the sinners can find life everlasting. Bliss, a preacher is a man who carries God's load. And that's the whole earth, Bliss boy. The whole earth and all the people." (Ellison, *Juneteenth*, 41)

The tragedy here is simple enough to understand. A preacher is not a god, and a boy, even one dressed in a white suit and preaching with all the fire and conviction of a thousand saints, is not a man. And even if he were, he should not, could not, stand the weight of the earth and all its people. Thus Bliss is broken.

And not even an ice cream, nothing to sustain me in my own terms. Nothing to make it seem worthwhile in Bliss's terms.

At Deacon Wilhite's signal they raise me and it is as though the earth has fallen away, leaving me suspended in air. I seem to float in the blackness, the jolting of their measured steps guided by Deacon Wilhite's precise instructions, across the contoured ground, all coming to me muted through the pink insulation of the padding which lined the bottom, top, and, sides, reaching me at blunt points along my shoulders, buttocks, heels, thighs. A beast with twelve disjointed legs coursing along, and I its inner ear, its anxiety; its anxious heart; straining to hear if the voice that sustained its line and me still soared. Because I believed that if he breathed while I was trapped inside, I'd never emerge. . . . Through the thick satin-choke of the lining the remote singing seeming miles away and the rhythmical clapping of hands coming to me like sharp, bright flashes of lightning, promising rain. Moving along on the tips of their measured strides like a boat in a slow current as I breathe through the tube in the lid of the hot ejaculatory air, hushed now by the entry and passage among them of that ritual of silk and satin, my stiff dark costume made necessary to their absurd and eternal play of death and resurrection . . . Back to that? No! (Ellison, *Juneteenth,* 142–143)

Of course Bliss's coffin acts most specifically as a metaphor for the womb, that comfortable, if dark and strangely confining, space from which the child must emerge. And as if to guard against his readers becoming lost in the process of unpacking his metaphors, Ellison litters the passage with clues: pink insulation, breathing tube, measured rhythmic movement, and most especially that hot ejaculatory air that figure not only the child in the womb but also the child vaguely aware of its own conception. This is, in fact, where the novel's critique becomes most harsh. It is obvious that Ellison means to edit Freud, to disrupt the familiar story of the son's rivalry and subsequent identification with the father precisely by seasoning Freud's narrative with elements taken from the black and American vernaculars. It is also obvious that the most significant of these elements, what one might call the unconscious of this text, is the memory of the Middle Passage or, more precisely, the memorialization of the loss of that memory. Bodies stacked atop one another marinating in their own filth; starvation and rape; innocents thrown into the Atlantic—these are all hallowed images in the (Black) American national consciousness. And yet no American has a memory of any such event. On the contrary, my ability to evoke these scenes with such alacrity has as much to do with the profit-driven motives of Hollywood and Madison Avenue as they do with any tradition of tales of horror whispered from generation to generation, from proud father to anxious son.

Ellison's critique then, what I have called his pessimism, turns on the reality that though Americans are in the remarkable position of having an extremely well-documented account of our origins, we continue, especially in moments of great piety, to insist upon the trivialization of that history, that originality, by placing it within an impossibly simplistic frame in which there are winners and losers, masters and slaves, heroes and victims, straights and queers. What we forfeit, in the process, is a rich sense of our history, an awareness of that everyday churning of body against body, belly against belly, the understanding that our nation's development has not been simply a matter of faceless political machinations or amoral economic motives. Instead we are a nation that for better or worse has had its traditions secured by individuals, many simple, some cruel, and a few heroic, but individuals all the same. The crime that we see enacted in this passage then is that (black) individuality has been subsumed to black tradition. Bliss is put to the service of rearticulating *the* primary conceit of Black American culture, that our community, our history and traditions, are the evidence of life's springing from death. But in so doing, Bliss is suffocated. Indeed in our efforts to memorialize human tragedy we seem all too often to extinguish that vibrant, striving, unpredictable humanity that we mean to celebrate.

I would concur with Ellison on one point then. The continuation of a rhetoric of American national identity that turns on the presumed necessity of maintaining ethnic specificity (whites, blacks, Latinos, Asians, Jews) has the effect of deadening our national symbols. Thus the tragedy that Ellison pinpoints here is not simply that a congregation would engage in a gaudy ritual in which a child rises from a coffin in order to give substance to a people's dream of rebirth and redemption. Nor is it that this child's fair skin and presumably European features add a certain potency to the spectacle being enacted. Instead the tragedy is that this most sacred moment, this celebration of the human spirit, the return of the lost, the redemption of the slave, is always understood as an essentially parochial event. The Negroes are the descendants of American chattel, but there are no others. The Negroes celebrate Juneteenth, that day on which Union soldiers rolled into Texas with news of Emancipation, but they do so alone. Moreover, if Bliss, rosy cheeks, bright eyes, straight hair, were acknowledged as an "actual white person," that particularly American monstrosity responsible for the maintenance of European provincialism, then he would have no place in the spectacle; indeed the whole affair would be thrown into disarray.

I am attempting now to give critical substance to the notion of phoniness that is shot through Ellison's work and my own. I would suggest, moreover, that the belief that there is "a bit of the phony built into every American" cuts in all directions. Of course the white, especially the traditional southern white, is phony. Mammy raised and drawling, with a taste for black flesh that some might describe as unwholesome, *unheimlich,* all of his strutting, preening, and childish abuse of the Negro is put to exactly one purpose: the shoring up of the shabby lie of a distinct and peculiar white identity. The ridiculous spectacle of Bliss's race-baiting on the floor of the Senate is only the most comic instance of this in Ellison's corpus. The Black American, however, also comes in for his fair share of abuse. He has acceded rather too easily, Ellison suggests, to the false promise of superior moral status that is presumably attached to those who remain innocent; he inhabits too well his role as victim. Worse yet, this particular orientation toward American life and culture helps reestablish the most pitiful aspects within an already hopelessly self-deluded "white culture." Ellison reminds us that there are many who will go to any length in order to feel superior to others. He continues by suggesting that

> for far too many, "whiteness" is the last desperate possibility. Unfortunately, this need has become contagious, and now, as should be expected, certain Negroes, who for years have been satisfied to be merely human and stake their chances upon individual attainment, are succumbing to *blackness* as a value.[17]

One begins to see the vague outlines of a particularly odd, even uncanny, aspect of American culture. There is very little debate in the United States over who the real Americans actually are. Instead it is almost a ritual for good-natured citizens to readily concede the mongrel status of their nation. There is, however, intense debate over what genus and species of American one belongs to and where the proper lines of demarcation for these wildly important distinctions lie. As I suggested in the introduction, the "one-drop rule" allows the anxious U.S. citizen to move past the complex systems of racial categorization that one finds elsewhere in the Americas to a presumably more accurate, if infinitely less secure, conception of racial distinction.

Of course, all our musings about race rest on remarkably unstable ground. In fact, the very presence of the "blond and blue" Negro not only suggests sexual profligacy but throws into disarray the very logic of heterosexual reproduction at the heart of American foundation narratives. Thus we can only ever imagine a minority of persons as being "native" to our country precisely because to acknowledge the essential *Americanness* of huge swaths of the "black" and "white" populations would necessitate acknowledging and perhaps even celebrating all that mixing of bodies and bellies that continues as the guiltiest of guilty American pleasures. Indeed it seems at times that we are a nation holding its breath, each of us afraid—and a bit hopeful —that one day a child will step out from the crowd to announce the obvious: the emperor (or is it the empire?) has no clothes.

It is my hope that the preceding arguments will help us understand better a simple, if somewhat stark, reality of American cultural life. Though we rather appreciate a phony spectacle, the clumsy donning of masks and the infantile emulation of exotic cultures, we nonetheless can be rather harsh critics, prone to breaking up a show that does not hold our attention. From the periodic riots precipitated by "bad" minstrel performances in the nineteenth century to the gun play that took place during screenings of the "urban" films that Hollywood released during the 1980s and 1990s, Americans have demonstrated a great capacity to become overinvolved in spectacle. We understand that there is something missing, a supplementary element that, if timed properly and pitched correctly, might turn kitsch into comedy, farce into tragedy. Ellison reveals several such moments in his text, but none is more potent than when a white woman appears in the black church where Daddy is preaching his Juneteenth sermon. She enters the sanctuary as Bliss is carried forward in his coffin, but she does not appreciate the solemnity of the moment, nor can she, it seems, take a joke. On the contrary, she enters the church in order to snatch the child—her child, she claims—from the grips of thieving, tacky Negroes.

> He's mine, MINE! That's Cudworth, my child. My baby. You gypsy niggers stole him, my baby. You robbed him of his birthright! . . . Then suddenly there she was, her hot breath blasting his ear, her pale face shooting down toward him like an image leaping from a toppling mirror, her green eyes wide, her nostrils flaring. Then he felt the bite of her arms

locking around him and his head was crushed against her breast, hard into the sharp, sweet woman-smell of her. . . . She was crushing his face closer to her, squeezing and shaking him as he felt his Bible slipping from his fingers and tried desperately to hold on. (Ellison, *Juneteenth*, 155–156)

The performance of this woman is of course just as phony as Daddy Hickman's. With those wide eyes, flaring nostrils, and that biting grip, she seems more a child's nightmarish version of maternal suppression than a proper mother. Daddy later explains that after the death of her lover the woman slipped into a spinster's madness, snatching first Bliss, then a Mexican child, then a Chinese one, claiming that all were hers. The incredible thing for anyone paying even the slightest bit of attention, however, is the fact that in her madness this woman comes as close as any of the novel's characters to speaking truth. For not only does her appearance work to return the repressed element of the unfaithful white mother; it also demonstrates precisely the stakes involved in the American spectacle of redemption. She returns us to that deadly, timeless struggle between ancient black and white combatants. And always the question is, "Who has a right to claim the moral high ground? Which of us has produced this image of innocence, dressed in white, rising up from the dead husk of a too hastily forgotten past?"

Those of you who are familiar with *Juneteenth* will recognize the novel as a *Bildungsroman*. Its central element is the difficult journey of a young protagonist from childhood to adulthood. He is sustained in this process, moreover, by the devoted efforts of an able, if not altogether moral, mentor, Daddy Hickman. And like many novels in its genre, *Juneteenth* is concerned most consistently with the development of the intellectual. Ellison asks how the apprentice becomes the master or, in the logic of this text, how Bliss escapes Daddy Hickman's tutelage to become, one may presume, the superior preacher. "There, there it goes. I could just see it coming—see the way he's got his head back and tilted to the side?" Daddy Hickman asks Sister Neal, sitting by his side in the Senate visitor's gallery. Bliss, dressed in the elegant guise of Senator Sunraider, is giving one of his signature orations on the promise of American democracy and as usual it is filled with disdain for reckless coons, a disdain relieved only by his outmoded celebrations of southern accommodationism. " 'Yeah—why, Reveren', that's *you*! He's still doing you! Oh, my Lord,' he heard her moan, 'still doing you after all these years and yet he can say all those mean things he says'" (Ellison, *June-teenth*, 34).

The gods look down with pity on young Prometheus. For they recognize that the senator, this mortal who would raid the sun itself, understands the form of the gift he has taken but cannot, will not know its substance. After that last garish Juneteenth celebration, after being trapped inside his coffin then ripped out by a crazed woman who claimed to be his mother, after watching female saints, many black and one white, pull and scratch, bite and curse, all in the name of claiming his fragile white body, Bliss does understand the form of Daddy Hickman's gift. He understands that Daddy's performance is phony, just as is Rev. Eatmore's, the first man Bliss heard speak of the human desire to reach then raid the sun, the same man whose breath smelled of cinnamon and corn liquor as Bliss kneeled before him to take his turn in the pulpit. But still he does not know its substance. "I guess that must have been my first mistake with you," Daddy admits.

> It wasn't my teaching you the art of saving souls before you were able to see that it wasn't just a bag of tricks. . . . No, it was that I refused to let you have a *payment*. . . . You coulda saved more souls than Peter, but you got it in your mind that you had a right to be paid. . . . It wasn't that I begrudged you the ice cream Bliss. It was just that you wanted it as a payment. But that was my first mistake and yours too. Now you take that preacher, he probably took that drink of corn to help him reach up to the glory of the Word, but he took it *before* he preached, Bliss. And that made it a tool, an aid. It was like the box, or my trombone. But you now, you wanted the ice cream *afterwards.* Everytime you preached you wanted some. If you said, "Amen," you wanted a pint. (Ellison, *June-teenth*, 110–111)

Ellison rightly dismisses out of hand the silly notion that what is "wrong" in America is our tendency to play along the surface of things, to improvise, indeed to carry matters of history lightly. The master, alone in his study, perhaps overlooking the Campo di Fiori, seems to be not the least bit troubled by the fact of American phoniness, New World shallowness. We are a country that enjoys, indeed thrives upon, spectacle, and if it takes the clever manipulation of smoke and the careful arrangement of mirrors to pull off the desired effect, then so be it. I should rush to remind you, however, that Ellison was exceptionally concerned with matters of morality. Indeed his calls for individual responsibility were perhaps the most eloquent to be produced in our country since those of Ralph Waldo Emerson himself. We see then two warring ideals: Huck and Jim, Bliss and Daddy, Robert Park and Ralph Ellison. On the one hand, there is a sort of necessary phoniness: Huck's "ownership" of Jim, Daddy's of Bliss, and Park's of everything that is Negro. On the other hand, Ellison imagines that the grotesque American tendency to confuse human beings with commodities might be tempered by a set of moral commitments that presumably would preempt the all-too-common American desire to be paid.

This, however, is where the trouble begins. For though Daddy's breath does not smell of cinnamon and corn liquor, it does carry with it the stink of cowardly deception. His critique of his protégé is accurate. Bliss values ice cream more than his abilities to inspire a congregation, indeed to save souls. Still, Daddy forgets the equally potent critique of himself. Daddy values the saving of souls more than the saving of an individual life, the saving of Bliss. He has forgotten what Reverend Eatmore certainly has not, that clumsy piece of folk theology that stands back snickering at all our high-minded en-treaties to God: the soul is dead in the absence of the body. Trapped in a cof-fin, assaulted by hysterical women, and denied ice cream all in the same day, Bliss has come to embody the very essence of the Black American critique of these United States. Our countrymen (nay, our kin) could not, would not ac-knowledge our humanity, our history, our unknown future. The crime that was committed against us then is not so much that we were understood as things but, on the contrary, as walking ideas somehow come to life.

II

I propose that we view the whole of American life as a drama acted out upon the body of a Negro giant, who lying trussed up like Gulliver, forms the stage and the scene upon which and within which the action unfolds. If we examine the beginning of the Colonies, the application of this view is not, in its economic connotations at least, too far-fetched or too difficult to see. For then the Negro's body was exploited as amorally as the soil and the climate. It was later, when white men drew up a plan for a democratic way of life, that the Negro began slowly to exert an in-fluence upon America's moral consciousness. Gradually he was recog-nized as the human factor placed outside the democratic master plan, a human "natural" resource who, so that white men could become more

human, was elected to undergo a process of institutionalized dehumanization.

—Ralph Ellison, *Shadow and Act*

I invite you to imagine, just for a moment, that all that has gone before was
in reality a dream, the sweaty nightmare of a man, perhaps a black man, a
man who has lost a brother, a mother, a lover, a wife. I ask you to imagine
that he reaches a point in that dream at which he takes the best of what he
is, perhaps the ecstasy blaring out of the bell of a beaten-up trombone, and
like a god breathes life into it, creates from it a thing better than it was, a
thing destined to heal the country and lead the people. What would happen
to that man and that thing? Would the thing grow? Would the man? In this
way one might see clearly the secret that is Bliss. Though he is no giant, he
is, in fact, a monster. Though he is not trussed up like Gulliver, he is tied
down, entombed as it were, so that others might become more human. He
represents an odd, grotesque return of the colonial slave whose body was
exploited as amorally as the soil and climate—odd because he was first exploited by black men not white, grotesque because he escaped his masters
and learned to crack the whip himself.

It is no surprise that Bliss makes his escape through the vehicle of film.
Indeed film operates in American culture to perform two exceedingly important, if somewhat decadent, tasks. First, it operates, or so we are told, as the
great leveler. Within film, immigrants become natives, Jews gentiles, Catho-
lics Protestants, and it is whispered that even the Negro becomes white. Or
to turn again to a piece of bawdy American humor, in the dark (particularly
the dark of the movie house) we are all the same color. Second, in producing
all these transformations, film graphically enacts our preoccupation with
miscegenation, but in a manner that renders it acceptable, denatured if you
will, precisely by privileging the knowledge that what we are witnessing is
spectacle. "It *is after all* only a movie!" Daddy Hickman reminds Bliss of just
this as he carries him up telltale piss-stained stairs and into the cramped Negro section overlooking the proud white heads sitting in neatly ordered rows
below:

> Yes, you're going to be bug-eyed with excitement; but I'm telling you
> right now that it's one of those pleasures we preachers have to leave to
> other folks. . . . Too much looking at those pictures is going to have a lot
> of folks raising a crop of confusion. The show hasn't been here but a

short while but I can see it coming already. Because folks are getting themselves mixed up with those shadows spread out against the wall, with people that are no more than some smoke drifting up from hell or pouring out of a bottle. So they lose touch with who they're supposed to be, Bliss. They forget to be what the Book tells them to be—and that's in God's *own* image. (Ellison, *Juneteenth*, 222–223)

Of course Daddy is preaching here, but as I have intimated already his efforts to educate Bliss might be recognized as an attempt to effect a sort of desperately strict self-discipline. Daddy has reached a moment of crisis. He must concede to Bliss's desires, at least for a time, if he is to continue his work, but in doing so he must also acknowledge the very heart of their conflict. If Bliss—and Daddy—come to understand the complicated relationship between man and image, shadow and act, that stands at the heart of modern subjectivity, then they will necessarily have to ask whether these phony projections are not, in fact, the cement that binds together not only performer and audience, minister and congregation, but also man and God.

Ellison is again on remarkably dangerous ground. For the intellectual who rejects the moral equivocations of the existentialists finds himself working without a net. He cannot continue with the romantic racialism that he sees so clearly in his adversary, Robert Park, a racialism that I have argued is nonetheless quite evident in Ellison's own work. Still, I believe that the evidence provided to us by *Juneteenth* suggests that Ellison was testing himself during those many years of literary stardom cum intellectual isolation. I would, therefore, push the envelope of Jerry Watts's necessary critique of Ellison a bit by suggesting that though it is indeed true, as Watts suggests, that the roots of Ellison's aesthetic lie in philosophical traditions first articulated by Herder, traditions that give place of honor to an unchanging and, therefore, essentially mute folk culture that needs the interposition of the intellectual if it is ever to become articulate, Ellison was much more aware of this tendency toward primitivism in his work than Watts allows.[18] With *Juneteenth*, Ellison reached the very point of radical relativism announced by Sartre, Camus, de Beauvoir, and indeed Wright, the point at which one recognizes that human ethics are not given to us by God, nor are they—and this is indeed a quite dangerous insight for any writer—secured by the Book. Instead they operate precisely at the level of human will. We do what is correct because we choose to do so. But as Bliss and indeed Daddy demonstrate, we might—and do—choose otherwise.

I will expand my earlier arguments about film then to add that what is at stake here is not only the (homoerotically charged) relationship between Daddy and Bliss but also, I argue, the relationship between Ellison and an aesthetic apparatus that like Bliss was gaining independence, taking on a life of its own, becoming insistent. One of the obvious points that one can make about a writer who is as much associated with music as Ellison is but who expends so much energy in his "unwritten" novel thinking about the subject of film is that he is playing with the question of not simply how the artist might reproduce himself but instead how the *hyper*modern artist might do so. Once the tools of one's art are no longer the horn, nor the orchestra, nor even pen and paper—that is to say, once the act of producing is abstracted even further from the body of the producer, once artist and art are denatured—then what is one to make of the status of those presumably timeless values that attach themselves to the folk and are given new life in the modern world through the interposition of the intellectual? How then does the intellectual reproduce himself?

Again for Ellison these questions are worked out through the vehicle of perverse sexuality. Bliss's life might, in fact, be narrated as but a long series of thwarted, perverse scenes of heterosexual intimacy. Daddy receives the child without even, he informs us, "a few minutes of pleasure or relief" (Ellison, *Juneteenth*, 303). Once he has Bliss, moreover, he can no longer connect with a woman as he once could; he becomes an ever-suspect bachelor, a queer, tramping around with an (at least) half-white child. More to the point, Bliss himself becomes somehow detached from the funky and wonderful mysteries of life. He becomes, as I have argued above, less a little boy with a little boy's body and a little boy's needs and more an idea, a dream, the bliss carried in on the shoulders of a traveling preacher. Thus when Daddy delivers him into the hands of a beautiful brown woman to be cared for in the immediate aftermath of the Juneteenth debacle, he ends his day, a day full of ripe watermelons, cool well water, and the casual intimacy a woman might give a frightened child, next to her in bed, her nightgown barely hiding the mystery of her body, and yet he is not satisfied. Indeed this lovely moment, this tableau given to Bliss like ice cream long after the difficult work of saving souls has been done, can only frustrate him. It can only remind him of what he lacks, that thing that calls to him as he lies there kissing her softly on the cheek and whispering, "Mother . . . you are my mother," only to find himself unraveling in the face of the depth of emotion that he has touched in himself so that the scene ends with Bliss in the most pathetic of postures, a corner of the sheet stuffed into his mouth as fat, salty tears roll silently down alabaster cheeks (Ellison, *Juneteenth*, 191).

The demon that Bliss faces here, a demon that he will later obsessively confront in the comforting darkness of the forbidden movie house, is the same one who lurks within the deceptively simple riddle that drives the theoretical engines of this study, the same riddle that bedevils Ellison himself: "Once you go black you never go back?" There in the darkness, the beauty of black femininity laid out before him, Bliss has a choice to make. Will he allow himself the pleasures of the black folk among whom he finds himself, or will he strike out for the territory, as it were, turn himself into another ungainly limb of that ever-expanding, ever-consuming American monster, whiteness? We of course already know the answer. Bliss does leave Daddy. We also know exactly how he manages his escape. He picks up a camera and, in the process, transposes Daddy's carefully crafted technique into a more modern register.

What is still left to be answered, however, is why. Even after Bliss has become that most phony of phony Americans, the movie maker, one might still ask why he cannot allow himself the simplest of human comforts, that necessary intimacy of animal mingling, body against body, belly against belly.

> I watched her, thinking wildly. What would happen to this natural grace under coaching? With a formal veil placed between it and the sharp world and all the lessons learned and carried out with this natural graciousness to warm the social skills? Not a light against a screen but for keeps, Newport in July, Antibes with the proper costumes. Saratoga. Could she fly right? With a sari, say, enfolding her girlish charm? What if I taught her to speak and not to speak, to parry in polished tone the innuendoes dropped over cocktail crystal? To master the smile in time that saves lines? With a diamond of a certain size on that slender hand. Or an emerald, its watery green in platinum against the peach-brown skin. Who blushed this peach? . . . did the blight I brought begin in fantasy? There was a part in her black hair; her scalp showed clearly through. (Ellison, *Juneteenth*, 71)

Ellison offers his readers a rather deceptively simple menu of irony. It is clear that he means to indict Bliss for his inability to make love and to be loved, for his obsession with veils, costumes, saris, polished tones, and emeralds set in platinum, all of which are spoiled by the glimpse of scalp peeking out from beneath parted hair. What is equally as clear for the careful student of Ellison's delicious prose, however, is the fact that his own efforts to celebrate and critique the phoniness that operates as a vital part of American culture are so powerful, so utterly convincing, that one cannot simply shake one's head in dismay at Bliss's failures, his typically American weaknesses. Instead one must necessarily wonder at the phoniness conveyed even by "natural" grace, "girlish" charm, and especially the "peachiness" of that brown skin. When Bliss makes love to the girl, one might properly ask, What has happened to his body? What has happened to the man who hides behind the finely wrought mask of the small-time movie maker? Indeed we are all forced to wonder whether any of us can ever be said to truly remove our masks, to relinquish our all-too-American phoniness.

I began this chapter by asking simply how it is that Ellison's aesthetic, an aesthetic that I am readily willing to admit draws heavily from American traditions of blues and jazz, might have contributed to his inability to publish a second major work of fiction in his lifetime. I will begin to bring it to a close by making an admission that ought rightfully to embarrass any well-trained, well-established critic. I liked the novel. Even though one can find passages within it that seem unfinished or underdeveloped, I found the work to be a breathtaking piece of literature, one that spoke to me as much, if not more so, than did *Invisible Man*. Thus I would suggest to you that precisely the wrong accusation to throw at Ellison is that he was unwilling, during the long years since the publication of his first novel, to face a new set of demons, the reality of his own celebrity chief among them. Instead the power of this work is that one sees Ellison clearly confounded by the reality that he has forced himself to acknowledge. Not only is there no blues literature per se, a claim with which I believe Ellison himself would have readily concurred, but also the folk traditions that Ellison so celebrates, the very source of his own deep commitment to ethics and humanism, can no longer be recognized by any rigorous intellectual as either the exclusive property of the Black American or even as emanating exclusively from the folk.

Indeed in *Juneteenth* Ellison has demonstrated the awkwardness, if not the ridiculousness, of many of his own claims. His papering over President Johnson's blunders in Vietnam with a rhetoric of solidarity with a fellow "southerner" and soldier in the struggle for civil rights, his dismissal of those who would confuse the "Negro revolution" with the "sexual revolution," his depiction of life in Harlem as but a surreal masquerade, and most especially his purported preferences for the "unrhetorical activities" of simple farm people as opposed to the efforts of "big shot word artists"—all these evocations of the pastoral simplicity of folk life as opposed to the phoniness and neuroses of the city are thrown away like that unfortunate child discarded with its own bath water or, as Ellison would have it, like a blond-haired, blue-eyed baby discarded along with the trappings of white supremacy.

I will make one final point before I close this chapter. I have argued that the rhetorics on display here were structured by and through successive layers of homoerotic exchange: Ralph Ellison, Robert Park, Richard Wright, Albert Murray, James Baldwin, Daddy Hickman, Bliss. I will remind you that Ellison's efforts at reproduction, like those of the unnamed homosexual who so thoroughly haunts these pages, are always thwarted. Indeed what Ellison most clearly demonstrates in *Juneteenth* is the fact that the act of artistic production, with its emphasis on the individual, indeed on individual freedom of choice, is always and ever a denatured enterprise. The intellectual cannot and I would suggest should not reproduce the culture that has produced him. What Ellison vividly represents then is the fact that the endless reproduction of traditional culture is, in reality, as much a morbid celebration of death as it is of life. Thus when Severen, the child that Bliss sires by that peach-brown beauty, comes to the U.S. Senate and guns down his father, we are correct to interpret it as a moment of high-stakes cultural criticism, one that remarks not only the reality of Senator Sunraider's phoniness but also Ellison's. What Severen shoots at is of course the fact that the Senator is phony, denatured, indeed queer. More importantly, however, he has his eye trained on the reality that the same can be said of all American intellectuals, including those who most frequently announce their connection to the (black) folk. Ralph Ellison dedicates his bastard novel, the novel that should never have been published, to "That Vanished Tribe into Which I was Born: The American Negroes." Thus Ellison sounds one last blue note not so much for a vanished tribe as for his own vanished conceits.

3

Alas Poor Jimmy

They serve you at the table, they shine your shoes, they operate your elevators, they carry your suitcases, but they are not your business, and nor are you theirs; their business is with the elevators, suitcases, shoes. . . . Not one of their words, not one of their gestures, not one of their smiles are destined for you; it is dangerous for you to go out in the evenings in quarters that are reserved for them; if you were to stop in passing, if you were to bear them some interests you would unpleasantly stun them and you would risk displeasing the other (white) Americans. These thirteen million men, who slip by your sides like shadows, are no longer slaves. More than a half century ago, the United States freed their grandparents. They are not all necessarily from the laboring class, yet the majority of them live in horrible misery; some are lawyers, doctors, professors, some manage major newspapers, but their recent fortune does not confer upon them any rights; they count as much as the elevator boy in the eyes of the whites. They refer to themselves as "third-class citizens." They are the blacks. Do not call them "niggers": you will insult them. They prefer the expression "man of color" which is from official use or that of "brown American," which flatters them, or, if need be, "Negro."

—Jean-Paul Sartre, "Return from the United States"

If a black is overdetermined, then to see that black is to see every black. . . . One is led to believe, for instance, that one can "have blacks" by virtue of having that black, that anonymous black. The black representative emerges. One seeks out black leaders. Black novelists emerge as more than symbols of blackness; they become blackness on our shelves, our curricula, our mythology.

—Lewis R. Gordon, "Existential Dynamics of Theorizing Black Invisibility"

this depthless alienation from oneself and one's people is, in sum, the American experience.

—James Baldwin, "Encounter on the Seine: Black Meets Brown"

I beg your indulgence as I take a moment to readjust the clumsy apparatuses with which I am attempting to demonstrate some of the finer points of mid-twentieth-century Black American intellectual "crisis." I ask that you forgive my obvious disorientation, the enervating vertigo that makes itself apparent with each laborious sentence. Indeed I fear that I have lost focus, relinquished rhetorical precision, as the damp, heavy cold sneaks into peach-colored rooms and a strange gray light plays tricks on the eyes and the spirit. I will attempt then, at least in passing, to defend my somewhat outdated interests in existentialism, to explain again why it is that I have returned so late to a failed and unfashionable humanism.

They serve. They shine. They operate elevators. They carry suitcases. They are not your business, nor are you theirs. Sartre creates a pristine, elegant taxonomy of the so-called race problem in which there are no black individuals, only black facts, black history. And even this presumably profound reality does not confer agency—or even will—upon them. Indeed all the trappings of human freedom seem beyond their reach. Their grandparents, sleepy, half-conscious mass that apparently they were, had no hand in their own manumission. On the contrary, Freedom came as a singular event, one for which they had neither planned nor prepared. No thought, no struggle, not a single human action escapes the horrible misery that they, the blacks, collectively represent. Of course, my readers will understand immediately that Sartre simply reiterates the centuries-long tradition of writing black individuality out of narratives of Western modernity.[1] He establishes, like Burke, Hegel, Freud, Marx, and many others, a humanist discourse in which blackness stands as a sort of absolute boundary, the place at which even the most rigorous logic falls apart.

What is pitiful though, what wounds the contemporary critic, is that existentialism, at least in its finest iterations, is established on the assumption of innate, if not exactly unassailable, free will and responsibility. Indeed Sartre imagines himself at the end of a long line of philosophers who announced and privileged the human subject, the individual, as the primary—the only—agent of history and culture. That he loses his nerve in the face of all those black waiters and porters suggests finally that he had not seriously considered the racialist structures that supported his projects. He does not understand that the structures of desire that he announces, those many "natural" preferences reflected by half-formed words, mysterious gestures, and averted smiles, have themselves been established and maintained by human subjects and not the nameless exigencies of history or culture. Thus I return to the "lost" project of existentialism because I see all too clearly some of the ways in which it operates with and within the very logics of white supremacy that so many of us are struggling to dismantle. Black individuality is subsumed within "the problem of blackness," a problem emanating from an opaque and hostile world, never to be safely entered by even the most well-meaning of white interlopers.

I am reminded here of the great edifice, monument to the country's imperial pretensions, that stands across from the building in which I work. Trimmed in neat squares of red that catch the eye like blotches of new rust, it daily attracts thousands of tourists, rich with Euros and Yen, their necks straining to take in the impossibility of the building, dull floor after dull floor, unspeakable wealth built on spectacular poverty. They stand all day, blond, brown, blue, blocking the thoroughfare like doped cows, examining some imaginary world through the miracle of mechanical eyes until impossibly black attendants herd them onto the double-decker buses that shuttle them through bustling midtown streets to their late-afternoon adventures. Sometimes for an extra fee they even visit the outer boroughs, presumably to witness the intractable race problem up close.

I would submit to you that what Lewis Gordon narrates as "invisibility" might just as well be understood as a willed lack of vision, a well-tended blindness that operates as the most significant obstacle in the way of our overcoming the lies of race and nation. Indeed it is my hope that by rejecting the racialism that invades the existentialist project we might just gain access to the radical humanism that Sartre, de Beauvoir, Camus, Nietzsche, Kierkegaard, and their students imagined but seemed never truly to realize. It is this desire, this focus on human subjectivity and individuality, that I have argued marks *Once You Go Black* as a particularly old-fashioned project, one that wears its politics on its sleeve. Moreover, the not-quite-decent rhetoric that holds this text together—that is to say, my unwillingness to stand like Sartre, in the position of objective observer, dispassionate witness, even as I sit alone in airy apartments on the inner edges of empire—is one, just one, gambit in my struggle to stress the necessity of our taking seriously individual (black) subjectivity in the production and reproduction of our various cultures.

I

I turn now to the work of James Baldwin because it demonstrates so clearly the deeply held belief that the efforts of Black American intellectuals must always be measured against half-baked notions of the representative and the typical. Indeed, as with Richard Wright, twentieth-century Black American intellectuals risked great hostility from their "publics" if and when they demonstrated true singularity of voice, when they produced work that did not reestablish black tradition. It is for this reason that so many Black American writers have been understood to have lost talent, or if you prefer, lost their profoundly intimate engagement with the vernacular, as their careers progressed. Indeed within these overdetermined ideological and discursive structures, the (peculiar) intellectual gains status precisely insofar as he is understood to speak for the folk. Thus Black American artists must always guard against the assumption that they have traveled too far from their roots, lost contact with those all-important original sources.

This helps us to understand one of the stranger themes in the now formidable body of criticism surrounding the work of James Baldwin, and indeed that of Ralph Ellison and Richard Wright as well—that is to say, the rather perplexing notion of the artist in decline. The idea, expressed by a wide variety of critics and several biographers is that early Baldwin, the Baldwin of *Go Tell It on the Mountain, Giovanni's Room, Another Country,* and groundbreaking essays like "Everybody's Protest Novel," was an author driven not so much by a desire to express the particular gifts of the Black American community as he was by the necessity of demonstrating that any people's struggles, its triumphs, and most especially its failures are examples of the difficulty that the modern subject faces in the search for community, intimacy, love. Early Baldwin is understood as humanist, cosmopolitan, and infinitely ethical even as his work treats of the mundane realities of people living in the most precious and peculiar of enclaves, particularly those of New York and Paris. Late Baldwin is another matter altogether. Here we have an author whose laudable politics somehow have gotten in the way of his pursuing more-ambitious artistic goals. Indeed *If Beale Street Could Talk, Tell Me How Long the Train's Been Gone,* and *Just above My Head* continue to be read either as evidence of Baldwin's having succumbed to the tendency toward highbrow sloganeering that many people believe characterized the Black Arts Movement or, worse yet, having lost control over his craft. To state the matter flatly, a man who pursues politics, parties, the respectful attention of too many large crowds, and the amorous attention of too many star-struck lovers cannot possibly maintain the rigor, the attention to detail, and the loathing of everything clichéd necessary for the serious novelist or any serious artist for that matter.

It is of course not my place to defend either Baldwin or his work, though I will say that each time I hear this characterization it seems best suited, if at all, to particularly naughty graduate students and not to one of the finest American novelists of the twentieth century. Still, the very persistence of this idea frames a theme of decline that is clearly present in the criticism of Baldwin, particularly late Baldwin, and that is indeed shot through multiple narratives of contemporary Black American literary and cultural history. I would argue, however, that though the tightness and delicacy of *Giovanni's Room* give way to the breadth and coarseness of *Tell Me How Long the Train's Been Gone,* this phenomenon is best understood not as a failure on the part of the author but instead as one aspect of his attempt to come to terms with the changing social, political, and ideological realities of the universe he was trying to map. Indeed apart from the intriguing details of his personal biography, Baldwin is an interesting, even indispensable, novelist because his career was so closely tied to the rapid changes that took place in the mid-twentieth century in relation to the question of black and American identity. Thus if Paul Gilroy is correct in his suggestion that the era of New Racism is now over, that we have moved beyond a moment at which any honest intellectual might glibly articulate race as either biology *or* as culture, then James Baldwin was surely among the first to herald the coming of the new age, even if he was not sure himself of what that age would bring.[2]

Just above My Head, Baldwin's last and longest novel, might properly be read as a failure.[3] In some five hundred pages Baldwin meanders over the sometimes shocking, oftentimes mundane details of the life of gospel sensation Arthur Montana, as told by his devoted bother and manager, Hall. It is Hall who informs us at the beginning of the novel that Arthur is dead, a device that any student of Baldwin will recognize from earlier points in his career. The novel is packed, in fact, with previously utilized elements. New York and New Yorkers, Paris and Parisians figure prominently. Drinking becomes the glue that binds together all sorts of unlikely communities. Various forms of sexuality exist rather easily alongside one another, while the entire mixture has been spiced with a healthy portion of Black American Protestantism. One might mark this as a failed novel then precisely to the extent that one expects originality, cleverness. This is exactly, however, what Baldwin seems not to have been attempting.

Instead, writing at the close of what one might call the hot portion of the modern civil rights movement (that is to say, after the deaths of Martin Luther King Jr., Malcolm X, and Medgar Evers), Baldwin is concerned most faithfully with the passing of a certain sense of personal and communal intimacy. Thus the trick he plays on his most careful and intimate readers is to reestablish early themes in this late novel even as he insists that those themes can no longer sustain either the artist or the communities that produced the artist. That is to say, Baldwin has come to understand that the old intimacies—the intimacy of the church, of the racial community, sexual intimacy, familial intimacy, the presumed intimacy shared between the politically committed intellectual and the people whom he serves—can no longer and indeed never could be certain. I would argue, in fact, that Baldwin's warning is that the presupposition of intimacy, the assumption that one truly knows and indeed has always known one's interlocutor, is often a terrible and deadly gambit in that it robs the beloved of the ability to choose, to opt out.

Perhaps I can clarify what I am attempting to articulate by turning to what I believe to be one of the least questioned discourses of intimacy within American culture. It is almost a reflex action for the Black American, particularly the Black American intellectual, to express a close connection to his community, the folk. This intimate relationship is formed, one might presume, from shared experiences that are peculiar to Black American persons, profound experiences that only the most odd and perhaps obscene black individuals might miss. Thus one is never converted to blackness but instead is born into it. There is no choice of black identity and thus no choice of black intimacy. Indeed it comes to us from our forebears. I would argue, however, that in the absence of this choice the very notion of black intimacy is impossible to sustain. The black subject cannot possibly establish an intimate connection with his people because he is, in fact, not a distinct subject at all but instead a more or less standard emanation of a nebulous, undifferentiated black community. Indeed if he does not have a real option to reject the other (because he is not distinct from the other), then he also has no real option to embrace it.

A perhaps more palatable version of this line of reasoning would treat of the manner in which presumably white persons often assume incredible knowledge of their supposedly black compatriots. The Black American continues to be a quite well-known quantity for many whites. He is often understood, in fact, as but another example of impossibly overdetermined biological and cultural legacies. Hall makes exactly this point when he speaks of the odd sexual attraction that many whites feel for him:

> I had made out a few times with white chicks, in this bar, but maybe I was growing old fast: I was fascinated, but left untouched, drowned in deep water, but came up thirsty. It must be admitted that I knew absolutely nothing, and was dragged around by the insatiable curiosity of my prick, which was an object of the most compelling curiosity for little white girls, as well as for their boyfriends, who literally did not know what to make of it. It was more a matter of its color than its size, or perhaps, its color *was* its size. I had lived with it all my life, and knew that is was, roughly, the same color as my ass and my face; and it seemed to be, as I usually was, big enough for whatever it had to do. But they always looked at it as though Napoleon had just dragged it up from Egypt, especially for them, and though they could make it as hard as stone, they also turned it that cold. (Baldwin, 88)

We see that at the quintessentially intimate moment, the moment of (interracial) sexual contact, the participants, the black and the white, become ever more distant from one another. On the one hand, white women and men cannot see Hall because of an enormous penis blocking their view, a penis so black it absorbs all color. Indeed Hall's face and ass can no longer be distinguished from his penis. The organ's blackness is so overwhelming that it has the ability to bend space; color becomes size, the man takes on the dimensions of the phallus. On the other hand, Hall himself, perhaps as a matter of self-defense, manifests this same tendency toward reduction. He does not speak of individuals but instead little white girls who are more or less indistinguishable from their boyfriends. More telling still, he relinquishes self-control to the penis, investing it with an insatiable curiosity that he does not possess.

I make this latter point in an effort to move us beyond the mistaken assumption that what Baldwin was after was the simple castigation of white racism and white racists. On the contrary, Baldwin moved in this last novel decidedly outside the arena of protest that he so rightly characterized as a trap for the Black American intellectual. *Just above My Head* is not solely or even primarily concerned with horrors faced by Black Americans or Black

American artists during the difficult transition years of the 1950s and 1960s. It would be more correct to suggest that the primary concern of the novel is the question of American alienation, the ways in which all Americans substitute highly articulate jingoism for intimate understanding of either our nation or the many people who inhabit it.

Even as I make this rather harsh claim, however, I want to keep in play the profound lack of pessimism that I believe is evident in Baldwin's work. For if it is indeed true that depthless alienation is the sum of the American experience, it is also true that this alienation is, in a sense, our birthright, the only basis we have for the production of a national culture. Moreover, the fact of alienation, the fact, say, that Americans tend to have such a shabby and thin understanding of the basics of even our most recent history allows us the incredible luxury of forgetting and thus of choosing a course different from the bloody path set out for us by our ancestors. Baldwin writes to southern whites:

> It's not *we* who can't forget. *You* can't forget. We don't *spend* all our waking and sleeping hours tormented by your presence. *We* have other things to do: don't *you* have anything else to do? But maybe you don't. Maybe you really don't. Maybe the difference between us is that I never raped your mother, or your sister, or if and when I did, it was out of rage, it was not my way of life. Sometimes I even loved your mother, or your sister, and sometimes they loved me: but I can say that to you. You can't say that to me, you don't know how. You can't remember it, and you can't forget it. You can't forget the black breasts that gave you milk: but you don't dare remember, either. Maybe the difference between us is that it might have been my mother's or my grandmother's breasts you sucked at, and she never taught me to hate you: who can hate a baby? (Baldwin, 352–353)

I do realize that I am on dangerous ground, that indeed I may be marking myself as that most pathetic of modern monstrosities, the intellectual who champions the virtues of anti-intellectualism. Still, in my own defense, I will point out that my goal here is to work through the rather underappreciated insights of the late Michael Cooke, who reminds us that forgetting was for the midcentury black subject not a luxury but instead a means of survival, a way of rearticulating the world that allowed one to "maintain a minimum level of stability."[4] I would add to this that this process of forgetting, or rather the process of decline, the process that I believe Baldwin narrates in this passage, is hardly a passive activity. Baldwin wrote the entirety of this novel after the bloodiest years of the civil rights movement, after senseless violence and death, after the martyrdom of little girls in Alabama. Thus when he exhorts his reader to forget, he does not seek to erase memory of past horrors from our consciousness but instead to effect a dulling of pain, antipathy, to disrupt the will for retribution that has produced so much human misery.

I ask you to imagine just for a moment what bloody, cataclysmic consequences there would have been if generations of Black Americans, faced continually with communal exploitation and personal insult, had not told one another to "forget it." The phrase implies an active relationship to one's history, an agency established on the ability to start from scratch, as it were, to re-member, in the fullest sense of the word, to maintain a consciousness of self and community that allows one to survive with one's neighbor whether that neighbor stinks of hate or not. This is perhaps the primary manner in which Black American persons can be said to be engaged in a constant process of choosing blackness, choosing a relationship to American history that privileges critique without insisting upon the destruction of either state or society. This is also the manner in which Baldwin's own thinking might rightly be said to be in a state of decline. That is to say, he refuses to take up the mantle of Black American nationalism that was then being so meticulously reworked by many of his contemporaries. Indeed for Baldwin the production of a workable ethics of American identity at the latter part of the twentieth century involved a willful, messy forgetting of the country's recent past as a means by which to allow for the establishment of a less barbaric future.

It is song and most particularly gospel music that acts as Baldwin's most potent metaphor for this process of forgetting and remembering. Arthur Montana becomes a gospel star in the mode of Mahalia Jackson. In the process, he forms a youth quartet with his closest friends, Peanut, Crunch, and Red, that eventually becomes quite accomplished, so much so that the boys are taken on a successful tour of the still-segregated South, where they become an indispensable element in the many civil rights rallies in which they participate. More important still, Baldwin saturates his text with the lyrics of traditional gospel hymns, many of which are quite familiar to American Protestants, all of which immediately evoke a powerful emotional response from those of us sensitive to the ways in which song is utilized to humanize the metaphysics of our religious practice, allowing a visceral relationship to a still-living god and to past generations of believers.

Shine on me
Shine on me
Let the light
from the Lighthouse
shine on me.
Let it
shine
on me!
Oh,
let it shine
on me.
I want,
the light from the lighthouse,
to shine on me.
I heard the voice of Jesus say,
come unto Me
and rest.
Lie down,
thou weary one,
lie down
thy head upon my breast.
Shine on me,
shine on me,
oh, let the light,
from the lighthouse
shine
on me.
(Baldwin, 265–266)

The explanation for the undeniable magic of gospel, most especially its incredible resilience, may be the simple fact that gospel presupposes a personal relationship with one's god, a relationship uncannily similar to that between lovers. We are indeed invited to imagine ourselves bathed in warm, soft light as we lay our heads on the breast of our forgiving savior, a savior who like a lover cares for us as individuals and not simply as wards or acolytes. The great promise of Christianity is that though we may now suffer, we can be assured that our savior, our lover, will attend to our most basic desires, including the desire to be caressed, protected, bathed in light. Thus gospel cannot dispense with individual personalities. The form requires real sinners in "real" bodies (picture now short, fat, black Aggie West) precisely because performance ties us both to the intellectual and largely textual tradition that is gospel while also providing evidence that God is capable of touching, physically touching, the individual bold enough to seek his embrace. This is why an entire generation of Americans found itself enraptured by not only the throaty alto of Mahalia Jackson but also her incredible hand clapping, the evidence of a *physical* ecstasy brought about by a disembodied god.

The many individuals who listen with rapt attention to the ethereal voice of Arthur Montana are thus witnessing an essentially dialectical process, perhaps the quintessentially dialectical process. They watch as the performer tries to utilize the gifts he has at hand to hold together the sacred and the profane, the body and spirit. Indeed though gospel performance is freighted with the trappings of godliness, one cannot truly appreciate or enjoy gospel without some awareness of the complexity and fragility of the performer. One must know, at least on the lower frequencies, that the singer's body is indeed as unregenerate as one's own.

I am reminded of brief, tittering conversations from my childhood in which women, listening to Mahalia, heads cocked and eyebrows lifted toward Heaven, would comment, "You know. They say she was funny." The point of course is that one cannot appreciate the music's sacred nature without awareness of the singer's worldliness. Baldwin makes this point abundantly clear in *Just above My Head.* Arthur does not begin to sing until he is thirteen, and as Hall reminds us, "He had not claimed to be saved. He had not been baptized. (He had been christened at birth, but that is not baptism.) And, yet, he sang—indeed, he sang, and there was something frightening about so deep and unreadable a passion in one so young" (Baldwin, 75–76). Significantly, the mystery of the young boy's passion had been revealed already for the reader. Arthur relates to his brother a story, "a minor, adolescent misadventure, as common as dirt," in which he follows a man home ostensibly to run an errand.

> He said I was a cute boy—something like that—and he touched me on
> the face, and I just stood there, looking at him. And while I was looking

at him, his eyes grew darker, like the sky, you know? And he didn't seem to be looking at me, just like the sky. And it was silent on those stairs, like you could hear silence just growling, like it was going to explode! . . .

He took out *his* cock, and I just stared at the thing pointing at me, and . . . I did not know *who* to scream for, and then he put his hand on *my* cock and my cock jumped and then I couldn't move at all. I just stood there, waiting, paralyzed, and he opened my pants and took it out, and it got big and I had never seen it that way, it was the first time and so it meant that I must be just like this man, and then he knelt down and took it in his mouth. I thought he was going to bite it off. But, all the time, it kept getting bigger, and I started to cry.

A door slammed somewhere over our heads, and he stood up, and he put some money in my hand, and he hurried down the steps. I got my pants closed best as I could and I ran home. I mean I ran all the way. I locked myself in the bathroom, and I looked at the money; it was a quarter and two dimes. I threw them out the window. . . . And I . . . just started singing. (Baldwin, 47–48)

Arthur's narration of this episode does a great deal more than reveal the fact of his homosexuality. It also announces his aesthetic. He confesses to his brother that though he was not able to touch either men or women for a long time after the incident, he was filled with a "terrible curiosity" and that he was "singing up a storm" (Baldwin, 48). The substitution that takes place here is not as simple, however, as it might appear. Arthur does indeed feed that terrible curiosity, a curiosity of the flesh, with the pleasures of the spirit. The joy of that spiritual pleasure, however, turns, as I have argued throughout this chapter, on the fact that the body is always involved, bathed in light as it were. Indeed if Arthur cannot touch either man or woman, he might readily lay his head on the breast of the savior. The belief that the spiritual is dependent upon the carnal, that the traditional is dependent upon the contemporary, and more specifically that the most cherished of Black American cultural practices are mere rituals of form in the absence of the highly idiosyncratic needs, desires, and styles of individual performers is the very idea that I am trying to get at when I speak of decline as a major theme in Baldwin's work. Indeed as Judith Butler, Elaine Scarry, Peter Brooks, and others have so clearly established, the body and all it implies (desire, disease, impulses beyond conscious control) is indispensable to all efforts at cultural production, *particularly* those efforts that reach a high level of discursive abstraction.[5] When one speaks of Black American culture, in fact, one always references a presumably black body, a body that is always in a state of disarray and decline. My argument here is simply that Black American cultural practices are not effected in spite of this process of decline but rather as formal responses to this process.

I hope that it is apparent that I am specifically attempting to avoid use of the term *improvisation*. Instead I hope to move beyond consideration of the formal structures of Black American culture and toward a more direct examination of the questions of ethics and ontology with which Baldwin was grappling. I do not believe that Baldwin was attempting to demonstrate that a homosexual might add some new element to the traditional practice of gospel singing. Instead his pairing of homosexuality and gospel is first and foremost an effort to encourage the reinvigoration of an American cultural form precisely by disallowing the common sense that supports it. Though I may be accused of apostasy, it seems clear to me that Baldwin was attempting to produce a species of alienation in his reader, to disrupt the often precious manner in which we think about black and American identity. For Baldwin and for many others, gospel might readily be heard as the efforts of a frustrated, or perhaps not so frustrated, homosexual giving voice to his most base yearnings. In making this move Baldwin not only writes the sacred tradition of gospel into a narrative of worldly secularism; he also gives back to his reader and, in particular, his Black American reader nothing less than freedom of choice. Once our traditions have been sullied, once they carry the taint of an all-too-modern homosexual funkiness, it becomes that much more apparent that we are continually in a process of choosing whether and how to continue those traditions.

Understanding this might help us to read better a rather long and lovingly executed interlude in the novel in which Baldwin narrates the details of a twenty-four-hour affair that Arthur has with a white Frenchman, Guy. From the very beginning the relationship is framed as a form of escape for the young singer. He has left the dirty, difficult streets of New York, where his skin, hair, eyes, and nose make him an all-too-well-known entity, for Paris, where if he is not exactly an invisible man, he is certainly an oddity. Travel abroad operates for the Black American as a sort of respite from the more clumsy strictures of American racialism. Arthur is briefly lost in time. He has an odd twenty-four hours in which no one expects him and no performance hall is preparing for his arrival, in which he has slipped from the consciousness of friends, family, and admirers alike. This is when he meets Guy.

With those interlocked hands, looking into each other's eyes, each pulls the other closer, and their parted lips meet—thirst slaking thirst. Guy closes his eyes. A trembling begins in Guy which transmits itself to Arthur. Guy opens his eyes and stares into Arthur's eyes, with a kind of helpless, stricken wonder, not unlike a child's delight, and Arthur takes Guy's face between his hands and kisses him again. He is trembling in a kind of paroxysm of liberty. Kissing a stranger in a strange town, and in a strange upper room, and with all the world too busy to notice or to care or to judge, with Mama and Daddy sleeping and Brother out to work, and God scrutinizing the peaceful fields of New England, his past seems to drop from him like a heavy illusion, he feels it fall to the floor beneath them, he pushes it away with his feet, all, Julia, Crunch, Peanut, Red, Hall, the congregations, the terror of trees and streets, the weight of yesterday, the dread of tomorrow all, for this instant, falls away, but the song—he is as open and naked and questing as the song. (Baldwin, 410)

The equation that Baldwin produces here is delightfully simple. The desire of the body, that which is transmitted through trembling, kisses, and wide-open eyes, is not the same as the desire of the community, of tradition. Mama, Daddy, Julia, Crunch, Peanut, Red, Hall, and God himself all drop away as Arthur, giving himself over to an embodied will, finds himself in a "paroxysm of liberty." The expression of this will, a desire that will not be squelched, is, in fact, song in its most basic form. Though the singer may stretch his voice toward Heaven, it is his longing for his lover that animates the music we hear. Baldwin reiterates this point in the hundreds of pages given over to the hot, sexual relationships that Arthur has with Crunch, his first lover and accompanist, and Jimmy, his last.

Still, I would stress to you again that Baldwin was not attempting an explication of the great contributions that homosexuals and homosexual desire have made to all manner of Black American cultural production. Instead by bringing the homosexual body so centrally into narratives of traditional Black American culture Baldwin allows us another opportunity to understand the great level of self-creation that is part of our experience and indeed of the whole of human experience. He also opens up the possibility that the Black American might decide against re-creating himself or his culture in ways that seem not only familiar but inevitable. This awareness is exactly the crisis to which Guy brings Arthur, who comes to understand, in the arms of his lover, that his embrace of that most sacred icon of Black American tradition, gospel, has been a willed act. What Guy, this French veteran of the war in Algeria, models for Arthur are the ways in which sexuality, aided greatly by the telephone and airplane, allows one to accomplish that all-important forgetting and remembering with which we have been concerned. This is not to say that Guy is the first or only character to have despised handsome coffee-colored men in one context while loving them in another. Erotic choice often operates, in fact, as a means to reposition oneself in society. I remind you here of Baldwin's tortured character, David, in *Giovanni's Room* as he struggles with the erotic and social implications of choosing either "the white woman," Hella, or "the colored man," Giovanni.

Thus Arthur might also come to understand that he might choose otherwise, that he might not only reject gospel but reject the very common sense of what it means to be both black and American. Baldwin is rather explicit, in fact, about his belief that this interlude forces Arthur to understand that he does not passively inhabit his identity but instead constantly re-creates it. He writes of the singer's anger and confusion after hearing that Guy does not like being French and wishes that he could be something else.

> for the very first time, and almost certainly because he is sitting in this unknown avenue, he puts the two words together *black American* and hears, at once, the very crescendo of contradiction and the unanswering and unanswerable thunder and truth of history—which is nothing more and nothing less than the beating of his own heart, his song. In many ways, he does not like being a black American, or being black, or being American, or being Arthur, and for many millions of people, in his country, and elsewhere—including France—his existence was proof of the un-speakable perversity of history, a flaw in the nature of God. However: here he is, sitting on the Champs-Élysées, with Guy, a Frenchman, a stranger, and a lover, not yet a friend. He does not want to think about it, it will ruin the stolen twenty-four hours, and make his burden, already heavier by a day, much heavier. (Baldwin, 421–422)

The work that Baldwin does here is to remind us that the truth of history is not that the Black American is an inevitability but rather a contradiction. More important still, he is a contradiction kept in play through a highly particularized set of discursive practices, that song that Arthur comes to hear beneath the beating of his own heart. And as Arthur begins to recognize that he dislikes being black, dislikes being American, then he must also begin to question why it is that here in France with Guy on the Champs-Élysées he continues to *be* Black American. In this way Guy's rather innocent musings become a challenge. He offers his lover a choice, a means of escape, the ability for at least a moment, those brief twenty-four hours, to change the rhythm of his singing, to become something else.

The heavy lifting that Baldwin does here, his valiant attempts to demonstrate that the Black American, or at least the Black American creative intellectual, does indeed have freedom of choice, is important to the author precisely because it gives new vibrancy to the statement, "I *am* Black American." After their lovemaking, their confrontations, and their brief escapes from the strictures of two impossibly complex, impossibly intertwined cultures, Guy and Arthur make their way to a café on the Left Bank of Paris, populated by a motley crew of Parisians, North Africans, and Americans of every shade. There they encounter an ancient blues singer, Sonny Carr, who completely dominates the room with performance and presence. This moment in the text, though rendered almost as an afterthought, is I believe *the* great moment of self-realization for Arthur, Baldwin, and the many readers who look over their shoulders, the audience represented by that interracial cast within a Parisian café. Sonny sings:

> Water-boy,
> now, tell me
> where you hiding?
> If you don't a-come,
> I'm going to tell your mammy,
> you jack of diamonds,
> you jack of diamonds,
> I know you of old, boy,
> yes, I know you of old!
> See, see rider
> See what you done
> Take this hammer,
> carry it to the captain.
> Tell him I'm gone, boys,
> tell him I'm gone
> (Baldwin, 432–433)

Arthur sits attentively, enveloped in the spirit of a song that he has listened to many times but that he has never truly heard. It is of course a hail, an exhortation to Arthur and to all those whom he represents to pick up the hammer that Sonny has himself carried for so long, the same hammer that he had been exhorted to pick up long before the young man's birth. And it is in this moment that Arthur understands what it is to be a singer, what it is to be a song. It is not simply a matter of giving voice to a people's tradition, nor of demonstrating one's own genius. The song is produced at the moment at which the individual embraces tradition though he might choose otherwise; it is the acceptance of one's people, one's painfully American people, for better or worse. It is also a forgetting, a forgetting of all that drives us away from tradition (pain, degradation, boredom), and as such it is a necessary precursor to a remembering, a reestablishing of that tradition in another key. Sonny eventually finishes his song then thanks his audience, and with that gesture he gives Arthur the key to his own identity.

> Sonny bows his head before what his audience supposes to be his past, and his condition. He bows his head before their profound gratitude that this past, and this condition, are his, and not theirs. He bows his head before their silent wonder that he can be so highly esteemed as a performer and treated so viciously as a man: whenever, and wherever, he is esteemed to be one. He hears, in their applause, a kind of silent wonder, inarticulate lamentations. They might, for example, be willing to give "anything" to sing like that, but fear that they haven't "anything" to give: but, far more crucially, do not suspect that it is not a matter of being "willing." It is a matter of embracing one's own life, even though this life so often seems to be, merely, one's doom. And it is, in a way, though not "merely." But to refuse the doom of one's only life is to be trapped outside all nourishment; their wonder, then, is mixed with, and their lamentations defined by, that paralyzing envy from which what we call "racism" derives so much of its energy. Racism is a word which describes one of the results—perhaps the principal result—of our estrangement from our beginnings, from the universal source. (Baldwin, 433)

Sonny's work here is to bring Arthur back into the fold, for though as I have argued it is indeed possible for Arthur to choose a path other than that marked "Black American," it is also the case that for many individuals Black

American identity continues to be the most workable and ethical discursive strategy by which to negotiate the incredible difficulties inherent within the life of the modern subject, regardless of the color of the subject's skin or the relative kink of his hair. Arthur himself takes the stage—that is to say, he picks up the hammer that Sonny lays down. He also leaves Guy and Paris and returns to the United States and his Black American lover, Jimmy. The point for Baldwin, however, is certainly not to decry either the cosmopolitan or the interracialist but instead to reiterate that though he might have done otherwise, he, James Baldwin, Jimmy, has chosen to continue his love affair with that great mass of contradiction that stands between the labels "Black" and "American."

I have argued already that the black individual who does not have some understanding, however vague, that they might reject commonsense notions of identity, that they might perhaps re-create themselves into something unknown or perhaps unimaginable, is an individual who lacks full status as a subject. Indeed though I am old-fashioned enough to understand why it is that many Black American people recoil at the idea of others rejecting our most precious traditions, I must say that I am much more concerned with the ways in which the freedom to fashion one's own subjectivity seems to me a basic human right. Thus part of my effort is to expand radically our understanding of what we mean by freedom of choice. I believe, in fact, that this idea becomes entirely hollow if it stops at the simple freedom to choose what acts one might perform—or not perform—with one's body and does not encompass how one might *imagine* that body, that is to say, which discursive strategies one might choose to utilize in order to make sense of the body. Moreover, not understanding Black American identity as a process of choosing and re-choosing, or if you prefer, forgetting and re-membering, is to cheapen both our culture and our cultural studies. Black Americans become, in fact, bad, faint copies of African captives and not, as I believe is our truth, persons who have self-consciously chosen to stand for what is most correct and most noble in American society. Thus the insult that the contemporary Black American confronts is strangely enough strikingly similar to that confronted by previous generations of enslaved persons. We are a people who are animated. We can be seen and heard. We can love and hate, kill and be killed, yet it is still not the case that we are imagined as a community whose individual members have control over their own histories and futures. We are physically alive yet socially dead. We slip by like shadows even though we are no longer slaves.

I would like, at this point, to retreat a bit from an argument that I made earlier. While I do believe that Baldwin struggled throughout the entirety of his career to operate outside the precincts of what we loosely label "protest," it does seem to me that in *Just above My Head* Baldwin works assiduously to demonstrate the ways in which the Black American, and most especially the Black American intellectual, is not allowed the fullest practice of that most complex of modern activities, social life. James Baldwin was one of many Black American artists who achieved levels of success in their careers that they could hardly have imagined in their early lives. Baldwin, like his character Arthur Montana and his contemporary Mahalia Jackson, was adored by his public, but he remained ever aware of the fact that within the production and reproduction of this adoration some aspect of his personal life, his personality, if you will, was slipping away from him. At the moment at which the audience disallows the distinction between the performer and the performance it has in truth become hostile, deadly. Desire for the performer, indeed desire for the performer's body, is often not a desire for an *individual* at all but rather a simulacrum, a minstrel, the idea of profound tradition somehow come to life.

In a now infamous *Esquire* profile of Baldwin, an incident is related in which he is accosted by a black man, a stranger, at Smalls Paradise in Harlem. The two exchange words, and Baldwin is escorted from the scene, only to reappear a few moments later, jovial but clearly shaken.

> When Baldwin returned the tears were gone, but in their place was a jangling, lurching-doll quality, grimaces, overly intense looks, sudden inward disappearances and pointless smiles. He kissed too many faces, cupped too many heads in his hands, fell forward and backward into too many arms. . . . He moved or was pulled to different tables and different people, but he was not really *with* it, not *with* anyone.[6]

Though I think it right to point out that this profile reeks of the intense homophobia that was visited upon James Baldwin throughout his career, I also think that the piece's author has demonstrated, in a rather elegant manner, one of the more disturbing aspects of the cult of celebrity. It becomes difficult not only for the audience to distinguish the performer from the performance, the man from the jangling, lurching, grimacing doll, but also for the artist himself. And perhaps even more importantly, this text speaks volumes about the way in which the celebrity of an intellectual like Baldwin is all too often understood as evidence of that individual's having traveled too far from some original source. Thus what we see in this passage is a back-handed treatment of Baldwin's having lost something significant, having declined as a (black) writer precisely because he dared pursue an intellectual agenda that privileged so-called traditional black identity as well as his own peculiar choices as both a man and an artist.

Thus if Baldwin can be said to be making any protest at all in *Just above My Head*, it is surely the same as that made a century before by Emily Brontë: "I cannot live without my life."[7] The privacy and sacredness of the individual and the individual's body must be maintained even and especially at the moment at which that individual offers up his own life story as a potent metaphor for the reality and the promise of the human condition. This is exactly the warning that Baldwin offers us in two exceedingly difficult scenes. The first involves one of the most finely wrought female characters of Baldwin's career, Julia. We meet her early in the text, as a child preacher, one who seemingly is totally at one with her religion, her God. The girl's faith is shaken quite severely, however, by the deaths of both her worldly mother, Amy, and her spiritual mother, Sister Bessie. She is stunned by the crassness displayed by her community and herself in relation to the suffering of these women. Julia has, in fact, ostensibly forbidden her mother from seeking the medical attention that might very well have saved her life. That is to say, the girl's naive belief that God exists apart from human subjectivity and individuality turns into a sort of sadistic rigidity, an inability to accept either the reality of human intersubjectivity *or* the promise of an unknown and unknowable individuality. Indeed Julia's great sin is that she forgets the key lesson that stands at the heart of the gospel, the spirit is dead in the absence of the unrepentant flesh.

The collusion of Julia's father, Joel, in this disaster can be explained by the fact that the man has become accustomed to the comfortable mode of life afforded him by his daughter's celebrity. It also speaks, however, to the fact that he himself cannot fully distinguish performer from performance, little girl from vessel of God. Or to state the matter in a slightly more cynical key, Joel understands all too well that Julia's rigidity and her naiveté are indistinguishable, that the young girl's belief in God is strong but brittle. Thus when Joel eventually rapes Julia and initiates an incestuous relationship that results in a pregnancy and the destruction of what is left of his small family, the tragedy is not so much that the man has too little respect for the girl preacher but, in a sense, too much. He does not recognize or acknowledge that the girl's sadism is, in fact, a sign of her immaturity. Indeed he has accepted—or seemed to accept—her own underdeveloped version of Christian faith. God is above. We are below. He is spirit. We are flesh. In the one resides the very breath of life; in the other, only death. What Joel does then is nothing less than help his daughter in her efforts to kill the Christian God, to corrupt the erotic codes that stand between the shepherd and his flock. The savior that the two worship, the sacred creator that they celebrate, is so very ancient, so impossibly profound, that he has long since ceased to exist as a functioning aspect of human reality. Instead God has become an artifact, a thing to which one might genuflect but never a lover to whom one might retreat. Thus worship can be at best vulgarly antiseptic, at worst breathtakingly cruel.

> Just keep on doing it for me, he said. You keep on believing in *me,* we'll be very happy, we'll live off the fat of the land. . . . Nobody will ever have to know, baby, you'd be surprised; it happens all the time. Love is a beautiful thing, darling; something in every man, I believe, wants to turn his daughter into a woman. She felt his sex stiffen against her, and somehow, she broke away, for some reason she was terribly aware of the gray window at her back, and the yearning houses. *No place to run. No place to hide.* She knocked over the glass of wine, and the smell of the wine, the scream she could not deliver, nearly burst her brain. She fell on the sofa, and he fell on top of her. Still she could not scream. She knew that something in her had always wanted this, but not this, not this, not this way, she wanted to say, *Please. Please wait,* but he said, in a low, laughing growl, You and the Holy Ghost been after my ass *awhile;* you wanted me, you got me. (Baldwin, 147–148)

Joel violates his daughter to repair yet another faulty circuit. He is aware enough, sober enough, to understand that the girl's performance as a minister, her ability to invoke the Holy Ghost, is intricately tied up with her desire to please him, her desire for the father, but he does not and perhaps cannot understand that the very moment at which the girl's fleshly desire is trivialized, turned against her, she will by necessity lose contact with the spirit world that sustains both him and her. Joel's great error is that he does not understand that there is always a disconnect between the Holy Ghost and the vehicle of the Holy Ghost, the God and his horse.

Baldwin repeats this warning with the death of Arthur. The fact that the work's protagonist was already dead had been announced almost immediately in the text so that it comes as a shock when one reads the somewhat mundane death scene five hundred pages later. Arthur is alone in a London pub. This experience, however, is wholly unlike the twenty-four hours he spent with Guy. At this stage of his career he has become a quite famous performer, so much so that he begins to be aware of people staring at him; rather, he becomes aware of the people's eyes on him, particularly a pair of Irish eyes that stare at him in a manner that suggests both invitation and threat.

> He is aware of the unsmiling Irish eyes at the far corner of the room, is aware of the other eyes on him, and he wants to get away from here, suddenly, away from these people, these eyes, this death. For, it *is* death, the human need to which one can find no way of responding, the need incapable of recognizing itself.
>
> And then, again, something hits him, lightly, in the chest, and between the shoulder blades. . . .
>
> The journey across the room is the longest journey he has ever forced himself to make. He starts down the steps, and the steps rise up, striking him in the chest again, pounding between his shoulder blades, throwing him down on his back, staring down at him from the ceiling, just above his head. (Baldwin, 498)

The death that Arthur runs from but does not escape is precisely the social death against which Baldwin launched his unlikely protest. It is the death that surely would have met Julia if she had allowed herself to become trapped within her father's warped gaze. It is the death of the celebrated and the notorious. It is the death of those whom we seem to need so absolutely that we cannot help but consume every aspect of them—words, body, and soul—until there is no individual left. It is the very death that was suffered by the many martyrs of the civil rights movement, who were not so much despised by their society as loved too much, individuals who were not allowed individuality because of our tendency to forget the necessity of the body within the body/soul dialectic.

Still, I would remind you that Baldwin's *Just above My Head* is hardly a pessimistic novel; indeed it seems altogether hopeful. Hall, the advertising executive turned arts manager, lives to tell a beautiful story to his beautiful children. Julia becomes a model and eventually heals her relationships with those closest to her, particularly her brother and Arthur's lover, Jimmy. They all, strangely enough, come to live what many might think of as a shallow, even mundane, existence, but they do, in fact, continue to live. Indeed it is this very shallowness, one might even call it alienation, that gives them the ability to forget the bloody injustices that have been done them and thus to re-member, to reproduce a world that, if not more just, is at least a bit more comfortable. The incredible lesson for living that Baldwin offers us as Americans then is that we cannot always live alienated from our alienation. We must eventually come to embrace all that we are, including those parts of us that are shallow and perhaps even cruel if we are ever to reach the beloved community that we all imagine floating out there just above our heads.

Coming Back?

4

Saint Huey

> the self, taking itself as a work to be accomplished, could sustain an ethics that is no longer supported by either tradition or reason; as an artist of itself the self would enjoy that autonomy that modernity can no longer do without.
>
> —Michel Foucault, "The Final Foucault and His Ethics"

And so it seems we have turned the page—books, music, and dictionaries (American and Continental) all a bit tattered and somehow inadequate in the face of the heat, figurative and quite literal, that has flooded this bright and now somewhat less than airy apartment. *Once You Go Black* has grown unruly; it has developed (this was also its first year abroad) into a somewhat less than respectable example of Black American literary and cultural critique. It has become (with only the tacit approval of its author) a dogged, obstinate, and insistent queer. Indeed what is most certain as we begin this second part is that it is absolutely imperative that we recognize, refine, and build upon the rather shockingly advanced insights given us by that trio of mid-twentieth-century black intellectual giants, Wright, Ellison, and Baldwin, who reminded us early on that in the American context not only is it inadvisable and perhaps impossible to distinguish the black creative intellectual from the queer but also that so-called black freedom might be properly measured in terms of black culture's ability to allow for its own transcendence, perhaps even its own cannibalization. Daddy Hickman and Bliss, Fish and Aggie, Arthur and Hall (one could continue almost indefinitely) —these characters speak to us from the late and less-than-innocent novels of the great masters of a world in which the production of self-reflexive black subjectivity is achieved precisely through the rupture of tradition (or at least what passes for tradition) within Black American narrative. Moreover, in each instance the authors suggest that an overemphasis on tradition, memory, what I have called the profundity of Black American history and culture, has the effect of strangling that history, stifling that culture. Instead we all too often substitute static and overdetermined notions of a fully established subjectivity, one shockingly stable in its desires, for the everyday freedoms, body to body, belly to belly, of this great and dynamic world.

What Wright, Ellison, and Baldwin announce then is nothing less than the end of Black American innocence. If the discursive structures that we have examined thus far were specific to the twentieth century, that moment dominated by Fordist modes of production and the concomitant (re)structuring of our basic economic and social institutions, then surely one of the most significant markers of that specificity is the very self-consciousness that so typifies this moment. The black intellectual understands, in a sense, that his time is passing. He understands that there is nothing at all simple, obvious, or transparent about the notion of black peculiarity. Or to state the matter in a more positive vein, the most sensitive of Black American intellectuals understand that black subjectivity is a radically undecided concept. Blackness marks a site of becoming rather than a locus of fixed tradition. Thus the contemporary intellectual is brought to a moment of profound crisis. Indeed he confronts the existential vertigo suggested by Charles Johnson when he asks, "does it seem possible that the 'black experience' in literature truly exists only there—*in* literature—and therefore may vary from one author's viewpoint to the next, with nothing invariant in the 'experience' that we can agree on as final?"[1] What Johnson references is nothing less than the not quite fully digested understanding that Black Americans inhabit a particularly awkward position in relation to the much-referenced, if woefully underexamined, African Diaspora. Indeed we are at the end of the (black) line, yet the concept of diaspora loses meaning if our complex and contradictory experiences are not taken fully into account. Moreover, far too much of our cultural work turns on "the necessity" of our denying this basic reality. Our inquiries must, it seems, begin with a question (Africa) that is inevitably presented as if it were a final, irrefutable answer. In the process, the specifics of our experiences as Americans, the clumsy ways in which the so-called multiracial, multiethnic, and the multicultural are subsumed under the sign "blackness," are not so much forgotten as patently ignored.

Thus I would reiterate the historicist ethic that drives *Once You Go Black*. This is a text in which time matters. Indeed I have argued repeatedly that there is no logical manner in which we might assume that black subjectivity remains fixed throughout the centuries. Instead I suggest that the "blackness" that was arrived at in the course of the twentieth century was a radically different entity from the "blackness" that was articulated and debated in the nineteenth. Indeed even those partisans, particularly Black American nationalists of the postwar era, who most stridently stressed the specificity of black identity and subjectivity were met repeatedly with complexities of history and society so forceful as to irreparably undermine anything like certainty in the articulation of black peculiarity.

We would do well then to remember that one of the true miracles of twentieth-century American history is the fact that in the face of poverty, violence, disease, and racist hostility, all exaggerated by the militant conservatism of the U.S. government, Black Americans nonetheless experienced during the postwar era an unprecedented boom in their local economies, in their political and social opportunities, and most important for my purposes here, in their abilities to sell the intellectual and cultural gifts of Black American persons and communities within an increasingly globalized market, one with a voracious appetite for black performers and performance styles. This directs us not only to the question of how one might establish and maintain Black American singularity but also to the ethical dilemma that the transnational consumption of Black American culture produces. The moment at which the Black American becomes a cosmopolitan subject, the moment he is seen, heard, sampled in locations far from the red clay of North Carolina or the red brick of Baltimore, is the very moment at which he witnesses, or perhaps produces, the dismantling of the logic of Black American innocence.

As Stuart Hall reminds us, the very idea of an American popular culture is inextricably tied up with forms of style and performance thought to be specifically black. Once one understands this, moreover, it becomes particularly difficult to distinguish the innocent black from the guilty American.[2] It is this reality that I believe continues to vex a great many black and American intellectuals, many of whom have gone to remarkable lengths to erect and maintain the awkwardly structured binaries against which Hall warns us. That is to say, the continual articulation of black specificity, even as Black American culture is easily recognizable as cosmopolitan, transnational, and highly commercialized, is not simply a factor of racist oppression but also and importantly a means by which to maintain a rather potent ethical position in this country and on this planet.

We are, so the discourse of American racialism would have it, the blameless race. The black has been and is the victim of slavery, the casualty of segregation, the sacrifice at the altar of white supremacy. Black Americans are the people who somehow have managed to make themselves an integral part of the American landscape while escaping the stinking disgrace of having dropped bombs on Hiroshima or murdered babies in Vietnam. One might argue therefore that part of the reason for the continued reverence that many of us hold for civil rights and Black Power figures like Martin Luther King, Malcolm X, and Huey Newton is that their blackness, or their performance of blackness, allowed them to articulate versions of American nationalism that were not tainted by the ugly spectacles of intolerance that typified much of twentieth-century American life. To put it bluntly, innocence is seductive. As we saw in all of the preceding chapters, even as we revile the black, funny child, we long for its absolution, its ability to banish the great weight of history from consideration as we attempt to continue our own incredibly awkward social and cultural practices.

I would suggest, therefore, that the spectacular ways in which some Black American intellectuals of the 1960s and 1970s articulated Black American culture and tradition worked specifically to relieve the tension engendered when the black intellectual came face-to-face with the reality that his "race" was not simply a product of tradition and reason but also a sort of compromise with the oppressors. In this sense one might properly read many of the most strident announcements of blackness as surprisingly conservative attempts to deny the reality of Black American modernity. Moreover, as I will demonstrate below, one of the primary and most successful means by which intellectuals like George Jackson and Nikki Giovanni achieved these effects was to refer repeatedly to an ancient, indeed ahistorical, black body that worked to connect contemporary Black Americans to untold generations of Africans.

I

I offer these initial comments as a means by which to begin to make sense of my own rather complicated relationship to the recent history of Black American intellectualism and most particularly the history of Black American nationalist thought and political practice of the 1960s and 1970s. Much of my development as an intellectual has been, in essence, a self-conscious attempt to distance myself from what I take to be the excesses of black nationalism: its misogyny, its homophobia, and most especially its critical provincialism. Still, I find that even as I attempt to maintain an aloof posture in relation to nationalists and nationalisms I continue to be fascinated by the subjects that they treat, and more importantly, I habitually discover their rhetorics, their methods, their grubby obsessions within my own thinking and writing. Black nationalism creates the postnationalist progressive intellectual, and the postnationalist progressive intellectual creates the critique of black nationalism.

What I propose then is to disavow the aloof posture toward black nationalist thought, personnel, and practice that I believe ultimately leads us to political and theoretical dead ends. Specifically, I want to make sense of the odd slippage in my own thinking, and that of many Americans, that allows us to understand Black American nationalism as quintessentially performative (and thus almost painfully ineffectual) but nonetheless terribly captivating, incredibly compelling, remarkably seductive. Though we are perhaps further from the erection of the black nation in the twenty-first century than we were in the nineteenth, Americans continue to be absolutely beguiled by the memories of Huey Newton, Malcolm X, George Jackson, and the many other fallen martyrs of the nation that is not one.

I will proceed then by paying as careful attention as I can to the mechanisms that allow, or perhaps enforce, this slippage from the performative to the seductive, suggesting that at the center of this process one finds the question of innocence constantly articulated as a pole around which the issue of the Black American's ontological status is debated in late modernity. Thus one regularly finds in the work of Black American nationalists a species of theoretical denial, a tendency to collapse the Black American into a rather typically American conception of "The African," a figure overdetermined by his corporeality who nonetheless allows one to maintain ethical allegiance, if not exactly a shared set of interests, with the benighted continent, not to mention generations of the enslaved. I would suggest then that perhaps the greatest feat of Black American nationalist theorists has been their ability to produce narratives of Black American identity so focused on the tragedy of slavery and the fantasy of revolution as to encourage one to forget otherwise obvious differences between black persons here and there.

The work of Frantz Fanon motivates much of my thinking on these matters. For it is Fanon, the Martinican/American petit-bourgeois turned Algerian nationalist revolutionary intellectual, who understood as clearly as anyone the difficulty the so-called native intellectual faced as he attempted to produce a culture of liberation via the very structures of domination that he hoped to overthrow. That is to say, Fanon recognized the intellectual vertigo that I have suggested dogged many mid-twentieth-century Black American intellectuals. Thus Fanon does much of the dirty work for those many black intellectuals concerned with how one might struggle against racism and imperialism while remaining mindful of the fact that the fiction of certainty that one encounters in the appellation "Black American" is itself a primary tool in the enforcement of the white supremacy against which the radical black intellectual must struggle. Fanon writes of the antiracist, anti-imperialist intellectual project:

> the native intellectual over-stresses details and thereby comes to forget that the defeat of colonialism is the real object of the struggle. Carried away by the multitudinous aspects of the fight, he tends to concentrate on local tasks, performed with enthusiasm but all too solemnly. He fails to see the whole of the movement all the time.[3]

I would suggest to you that the straightforwardness of these claims, their lack of sentimentality, represents an effort on Fanon's part to shore up his radicalism, to place his critique in productive dialogue with the real world of anticolonial struggle. And in so doing, Fanon has first and foremost to draw attention away from the ambiguity and complexity of his earlier projects, particularly *Black Skin/White Masks*.[4] Indeed by insisting that the native intellectual is, in essence, too much the intellectual, too concerned with detail and local tasks, what Fanon does for Black American intellectuals, particularly those nationalists for whom the work *Wretched of the Earth* operated as a sort of revolutionary manual, is to move them away from full consideration of Fanon's claim that the "blackness" that envelopes our bodies and presumably connects us to Africans everywhere has, in fact, been provided by the racists themselves. Indeed it operates as a sort of second-order naming in which a slur is reconfigured as ancient truth.

> "Look Mama, a Negro."
> "Yes, Miss. Thank you very much. May I have another please?"

In this way, the proof of the Black American intellectual's innocence remains the very black body articulated so ably by that young French girl upon encountering Fanon's own brass-colored face. Moreover, I would suggest to you that the stridency with which many artists of the sixties and seventies continued the girl's articulations stemmed from the fact that, like Fanon, they presumably had to deny the complexity of black subjectivity, including black corporeality, if they were to get anything done. Aggie's fatness, Bliss's whiteness, Arthur's homosexuality all had to be bracketed if the simple relationship of contemporary Black Americans to ancient Africans was to be remarked and maintained.

Before leaving this point I should say that it is incorrect to assume that the ideological shift represented by the migration of our rhetorics from Negro to Black represents some sort of absolute conceptual advance. On the contrary, I would suggest quite the opposite. While the black body so ably described by postwar Black American nationalists may be a marker of a more politically efficacious political rhetoric, it also seems to be the last depository of wildly simplistic thinking regarding Black American history and culture. George Jackson, arguably the most sophisticated of midcentury nationalist intellectuals, makes the point nicely:

> My recall is nearly perfect, time has faded nothing. I recall the very first kidnap. I've lived through the passage, lain in the unmarked, shallow graves of the millions who fertilized the Amerikan soil with their corpses; cotton and corn growing out of my chest, "unto the third and fourth generation," the tenth, the hundredth.[5]

I continue to return to this rather stunning quote from Jackson precisely because the beauty and economy of the prose belie the incredible sloppiness of the thought. Jackson has no recall, no memory whatsoever of the African continent, the middle passage, enslavement. Indeed in his admittedly noble efforts to reclaim the lost African body he shuts himself off from the most basic realities of Black American history and culture. That is to say, confronted with the reality that there is no authoritative history of the slave, Jackson substitutes a sort of Baroque poetics of the black body—fecund modifier substituted for stale fact.

Of course what I hope to establish here is that part of the reason for Jackson's appeal is that he manipulates so ably the most potent trope within the production and reproduction of Black American singularity, the innocent Black American body. For Jackson, the fact of his body and the ugly response of American society to it prove that he continues as the innocent, combative African captive, unaffected by, if not unaware of, his captors' sins. Thus for nationalist intellectuals the most potent refutation of the Black American's status as native subject is enacted at the difficult juncture at which bodies are articulated through language. In the face of overwhelming evidence that there is no clear distinction between black and white bodies, we continue as a society, (non)black, (non)white people that we are, to insist on the most hackneyed forms of biologism in our political and theoretical discourse. This is as true, moreover, for the ostensibly black persons who are the victims of American racialism as it is for the presumably white persons who are its beneficiaries.

The question becomes then why it is that this fictional body, the body that is obviously produced through, if not entirely of, language, the body that speaks the horrors of the middle passage, continues as such an appealing draw for American intellectuals, black, white, and otherwise. In beginning to craft an answer to this question I have turned again to the work of Judith Butler because of the careful and clever manner in which she reminds us of the convoluted problem that bodies pose for philosophers and students of language. She writes,

> The body is the blindspot of speech, that which acts in excess of what is said, but which also acts in and through what is said. That the speech act is a bodily act means that the act is redoubled in the moment of speech: there is what is said, and then there is the kind of saying that the bodily "instrument" of the utterance performs.[6]

What Butler suggests is that the body, because of its excessiveness, because of the fact that it is both a subject of the speech act and the very vehicle by which the speech act is performed, produces a philosophical caveat, one that is particularly useful, I would argue, for those intellectuals most troubled by the question of who is responsible for the horrors orchestrated by modern society—American slavery and the long nightmare of segregation and racist oppression chief among them.

It is easy enough for me to suggest therefore that George Jackson takes full advantage of his putatively black body because of the fact that the blackness of that body (the hue of his skin, the tint of his eyes, the kink of his hair) helps disestablish his status as a modern and culpable subject. Moreover, the heavy-handed racism that continues in American society reinforces the notion that Black American persons, as evidenced by the fact of our black bodies and the incessant racist response to them, continue to be trapped in a premodern state, one that is by turns labeled "savage," "infantile," "tribal," "provincial" but that might also rightly be given the title "innocent." Calvin Hernton in his 1965 meditation on the American preoccupation with race tells us that

> White America perceives—or conceives of—the American black man as a "clothed African savage." White people—men as well as women—want to see the black man's penis. They want to see this "clothed savage" naked. The taboo against the "savage" adds to the temptation, and the fact that sex with the black man is "forbidden" makes it all the more exciting, the more obscenely desirable.[7]

I have no argument with the particulars of Hernton's claims. It is of course simply a matter of historical record that many white persons literally have been obsessed with the mysterious sexuality of black people. And, as Hernton also argues, some blacks produce whiteness as a sexual fetish as well. What I would suggest that Hernton misses, though, what he gets close to understanding but never quite articulates, is the fact that "blackness" is as much a fetish object for Black Americans as it is for whites.

Though the image of the clothed African savage is ugly and unsettling, this does not contradict the fact that it comes surprisingly close to Black Americans' (*African* Americans') own articulations of self. The idea of a certain unfettered sexual potency turns in fact on the notion of a camouflaged African savagery that has not only made its way into racist discourse but also into the liberationist rhetoric of black intellectuals. Again I argue that Black American nationalists utilized the specter of the clothed savage not simply because it suited the tastes of the white audiences with whom they were in dialogue but also because it allowed for the articulation of a Black American identity that was seductive and sexy because it was *in* yet not *of* modern American society. And in this way it provided a seemingly solid basis on which one might produce a literature and a culture of both combat and cultural renewal.

I would remind you that early in the twentieth century Charlotte Osgood Mason, perhaps the most significant white patron of the Harlem Renaissance, insisted that her protégés, Langston Hughes and Zora Neale Hurston, focus on the African and folk elements within Black American culture because she saw these as the only way to inoculate American society against the "artificial values" and "technological excess" that she attributed to Western culture.[8] Thirty years later, Mason's hope that an essentially innocent black subject would help resuscitate American culture would be repeated in a more perverse key by Norman Mailer, who found in the Negro's sexuality, his tendency toward violence, and his disdain for all things "un-hip" unbridled potential for the redemption of the country.[9] That is to say, Mailer, writing in direct opposition to Wright, Ellison, and Baldwin, puts the presumably psychopathic nature of the American Negro on display, arguing that through the example of the black's perversity one might find hope for a stale, rigid American society. Thus though for Mailer the Negro is cultureless, alienated, psychopathic, hated from within and without, he is somehow physically healthy and infinitely capable of fashioning morality, even and especially from the bottom. Because he exists outside of culture, because he remains inscrutable, innocent, he is powerful. Mailer's famous statement on "white Negritude" was of course roundly criticized by scores of American intellectuals. He was never, however, quite forgotten. My interest in Mailer stems, in fact, from the argument that Michelle Wallace makes in *Black Macho and the Myth of the Superwoman,* that "The White Negro" should not be discounted because it so clearly represents the depth of interest within this country in maintaining the notion of the innocent black, who in Mailer's hands, not to mention those of some of the country's most prominent black nationalists, easily morphs into the psychopathic black.[10]

> Nigger
> Can you kill
> Can you kill
> Can a nigger kill a honkie
> Can a nigger kill the Man
> Can you kill nigger
> Huh? Nigger can you
> kill
> Do you know how to draw blood
> Can you poison
> Can you stab-a-Jew
> Can you kill huh? Nigger
> Can you kill
> Can you run a protestant down with your
> '68 El Dorado
> (that's all they're good for anyway)
> Can you kill
> Can you piss on a blond head
> Can you cut it off
> Can you kill[11]

Nikki Giovanni's much-quoted "The True Import of Present Dialogue, Black vs. Negro" is a strikingly straightforward illustration of the ideology of black psychopathy cum black innocence. Giovanni's status as the unofficial poet laureate of the Black Arts Movement was based directly on her ability to articulate clearly the most pressing aspects of the changes in racial thinking then taking place within American society. The Negro was becoming black. The subject once formed through a set of enervating pseudoscientific discourses was choosing at this juncture to redefine himself in relation to an emerging black culture, a culture that was self-consciously antiwhite and, more significantly still, antinigger. It seems in fact that what Giovanni, an incredibly capable misreader of Fanon, was after was the disestablishment of the white/Negro nexus announced by Fanon. Giovanni seems only to understand, however, the most elementary aspects of Fanon's logic. She misses the fact that though the white has created the much-despised nigger, the production of a black identity that frames itself in contradistinction to this white-bounded reality still takes part fully in the discourse of racialism that Fanon helped make so clear. In fact, the bad black attitude that Giovanni invokes here, "Nigger can you kill?" is as much in keeping with the logic of American racialism as any display of black subservience and obsequiousness.

I have suggested that the innocence of the Black American, his lack of culpability, is what creates him as an appealing, sexy subject. I have continued in this vein by arguing that even when the black subject turns pathological, becomes the bad black, his antisociality, his niggerishness, once again does the important work of demonstrating that he is removed from the main currents of modern society and is, therefore, nonaccountable. I might add that my thinking in this regard stems from a rather willful misreading of Jane Gallop's masterful treatment of what one might call Lacan's performative style during his early-seventies seminars at the École Normale, in which he was consciously hostile to a nonetheless quite adoring and largely female audience.

> Lacan, inasmuch as he acts gratuitously nasty, betrays his sexualized relation to his listeners. The phallic role demands impassivity; the prick obviously gets pleasure from his cruelty. The evidence of the pleasure undermines the rigid authority of the paternal position.[12]

I think that the resonance of Gallop's thinking here with the arguments that I have constructed should be obvious. The seductiveness of the bad black stems from the way in which his hostility disestablishes authority, such that he becomes that much more available, personally, physically, sexually available, for the very audience that he castigates.

I want to say again, however, that my primary focus is not the way in which the pathological black is consumed or perceived by white Americans (though the continuing parade of black criminals, gangster rappers, and bad-boy athletes in American popular culture clearly demonstrates the necessity for a more accurate assessment of the racialized nature of the American libido). Still, my focus remains primarily on the uses to which those of us who self-consciously identify as Black American put the bad black, the undressed savage, who within Gallop's configuration is always already the feminized, domesticated subject.

II

> If sexuality is located . . . in nature, in bodies—in what, in other words, are the most literal and objective of realities that positivism can conceive —that is because sexuality is defined by its function, which is to ground the discourse of which it is the object. Without a stable object to study, there can be no positive science of sexuality. It is part of the function of sexuality, in its role as "a specific domain of truth," to provide an epistemological anchor for that science, a secure ground of knowledge on which the new science of sexuality can be built.
>
> —David Halperin, *Saint Foucault*

> It is therefore the idea of the Jew that one forms for himself which would seem to determine history, not the "historical fact" that produces the idea.
>
> —Jean-Paul Sartre, *Anti-Semite and Jew*

I would like, at this juncture, to change our focus a bit by continuing with the theme of intellectual celebrity that we began in the last chapter. Here, however, I will try to adopt a hopefully somewhat less shrill tone. Indeed to the extent that celebrity denotes particular genius or peculiar style I think it is most certainly a thing to be encouraged. What concerns me, however, what slinks mewling and whining around this bright apartment, is the clawing suspicion that the style and genius of the celebrity intellectual must always be negotiated in public. This is of course a rather obvious matter. What

I take to be a bit less obvious, however, is the fact that the media of exchange within these negotiations are the very profound traditions and sedi-
mented cultures that I am struggling, at least in part, to disrupt. The celebrity of the celebrity intellectual is a factor of how well he can manipulate
complicated narratives in which his particularity becomes evidence of the
profundity, the stasis, of the culture he presumably represents.

Moreover, as we have been at pains to demonstrate, much of this narratological magic is accomplished by reference to the (black) body or, more specifically, to that body's surface. As Fanon reminds us in *Black Skin/White
Masks,* one of the great accomplishments of late modernity was the so-called
epiderminalization of black subjectivity. In this way the narrative of the
black subject's "outside," his always visible blackness, trumps all others. "I
am overdetermined from outside. I am not the slave of the 'idea' that others
have of me but of my appearance. I move slowly in the world, accustomed
to aspiring no longer to appear."[13] It is not simply that Fanon announces the
fiction of a presumably "natural" visual distinction between black and
white. Instead what is even more striking is that with but a glance ("Look
Mama!") a whole world of meaning, culture, tradition, and history are ac-
cessed. As the black is an unchanging entity, the skin of any black stands in
not only for the skin of any other black but also for blackness itself. Thus if
the black subject moves slowly, this is but evidence of his attempting to
deny any quirk of subjectivity that would deny fungibility.

I refer you now to those many photographs taken of the founder of the
Black Panther Party, Huey Newton. Of course the best known is that awkwardly posed image of Huey seated in a wicker chair, beret cocked to the
side, a rifle in one hand, and a spear in the other. African masks have been
placed on either side of him, and his feet rest on a surprisingly kitsch zebra-
skin rug (see figure 1). The image is a study in the simplicity of nationalist
aesthetics. Newton's scowling face and his starched white shirt relieve the
monotony of his black clothing, particularly the shiny black leather jacket
that was the calling card of both Newton and his party. What seems to
be taking place is precisely the type of retreat from a full appreciation of
the complexity of Black American culture and history that I have attempted
to demonstrate throughout *Once You Go Black.* Wean a black man from
his enervating interest in modern cultural modes, including modern forms
of dress, and what one uncovers is precisely the African savage so ably
announced by Osgoode Mason, Hernton, Mailer, Jackson, and Giovanni.
Indeed, as I suggested above, Newton's celebrity has been secured by an

Figure 1

awkward narrative structure that would have all his innovations as a founder and leader of the Black Panther Party chalked up to his ability to articulate and reproduce the most ancient and profound aspects of our culture, no matter how fake these reproductions may ultimately appear.

Before I leave this matter, however, I would like to point to a later and much less well-known picture of Newton taken by the photo journalist Stephen Shames (see figure 2). This "domestic" image of Newton, standing in a well-appointed room, a large plant and a stack of books directly behind him, a Bob Dylan album in his hands, tasteful pieces of art scattered here and there, allows his adoring audience the intimate glimpse of Huey for which it

Figure 2

has so longed. Dressed only in white khakis fastened by a thick leather belt, Newton's broad, prison-conditioned chest is finally revealed for the titillated viewer as he half meets our gaze with his shy, boyish smile. The effect is electric. Here undressed, feminized Huey, "Huey the prick," seems to seek intimate connection with his audience, reminding us that (wink wink) behind the facade of leather jacket and beret is sensitivity, passion, and sexual prowess to which the formal dress of the Panthers gestures even while it hides the beautiful undressed body of Chairman Newton from immediate view. The point of course is to reassure the viewer, to remind him that even though the Panthers were quintessential moderns, master technicians of spectacle and media, their motivations were nonetheless base, corporeal, and indeed African.

Of course, as with James Baldwin's character, gospel singer Arthur Montana, Newton is an infinitely appealing, infinitely seductive figure. And just as with Arthur, what seduces us is never exactly Newton himself but instead the incredibly well-scrubbed surface that Newton presents. Indeed Newton is fascinating as a modern intellectual precisely because of the intensity that surrounded those many efforts to create, reproduce, and transmit his image, an image that I have argued repeatedly is built upon altogether simplistic and conservative notions regarding Black American identity, subjectivity, and tradition.

I mean, at this juncture, to suggest seduction (sexual seduction, the body's seduction) as an operative term in both the political history of Black Americans and, moreover, the ideological superstructures that allow for the production and reproduction of the Black American community. I utilize the language of seduction because it forces us to focus on the ways in which much of our political discourse turns on ideas of fixed, stable, and ancient black corporeality and desire. Further, I would push this idea to its limits by arguing that an enormous amount of our intellectual energies have been taken up attempting to discipline the so-called desire of the black subject such that when we look upon our lovely selves dressed up in pink, brown, yellow, mahogany, and blue we imagine that what we see is none other than the unchanging face of Africa. That is to say, the reason we still find pretty, redbone Huey Newton so attractive is precisely because he seems so savage.

If one takes seriously the claims with which I opened this chapter, that Black American identity at the latter part of the twentieth century has not only been performed but self-consciously so, not simply consumed but consumed on a worldwide scale, then it becomes clear that the Black American runs the risk of getting away from himself, of becoming something other than black. Seduction operates within Black American intellectualism as a check on this tendency by returning us to the discourse of black innocence that is revealed by the undressed black body. When crowds of Black American persons chanted the phrase "black is beautiful," they of course were being introduced to an aesthetic in which dusky skin and kinky hair might be favorably compared with the most flaxen of locks, the rosiest of cheeks, but they were also being initiated into a conception of history that would produce the innocent black body as one of the few sites at which one might locate beauty within our troubled nation.

This brings us again to the figure of a Huey Newton, infinitely available for women on at least three continents but sexually absent for his closest confidante, Elaine Brown, a woman hand-picked by Newton to take charge of the Black Panther Party during his long exile in Cuba. I must rush to make the point that by no means am I attempting to imply that I have specific knowledge of their relationship, their psychologies, the reality of their sexual appetites, or what have you. Instead, I am fascinated by the couple precisely insofar as they represent a rather intriguing problematic for students of twentieth-century black radicalism. I am stunned, in fact, that Newton was so careful to maintain a chaste relationship with Brown within an organization, the Black Panther Party, that actively promoted the fact of its leaders' physical beauty, not to mention the physical beauty of all black persons.

I would suggest, in this regard, that Newton was unusually aware of the manner in which sex and sexuality operated in not only the functioning of his organization, his movement, but also the articulation of his community and race. That is to say, Newton understood that his ability to seduce us all involved his remaining focused on the many important political uses to which his self-consciously constructed image was being put while leaving off consideration of the many blunt silences that underwrote this same image. Newton, like Fanon, understood that the good revolutionary was all too infrequently the good intellectual. Brown reports a rather arresting moment, when near the end of a trip to Havana to see an exiled Newton, she meets him in a hotel room so that the two might reconfirm their adoration for one another.

> "You're late." . . . "I'm leaving in the morning, you know."
> "Don't leave me." He kissed me on the cheek.
> "Don't be flip with me. I'm the one who loves you."
> "But why do you love me?"
> "Because you've got some good pussy."
> "Don't I though."[14]

The joke here is indeed no joke at all. Huey Newton, as leader, as seducer, as the quite visible figurehead around whom one of the country's most impressive black organizations was formed, as the crown prince of Black American radicalism, had extremely good pussy, at least so far as the term bespeaks an ability to arouse, to stimulate, to whet the appetite, and to bring one to radical self-awareness.

I believe then that Newton's reticence to give himself up to Brown, to allow the baser machinations of the seductive to enter their relationship, stemmed from an awareness that just as the performer loses some part of his individuality in the performance, the seducer always forfeits some part of the self in the act of seduction. The Huey Newton who seduced an entire planet, the Newton whose bed was hot with lovemaking, was indistinguishable from Eldridge Cleaver, Bobby Seale, or even the more chaste George Jackson and Malcolm X. One bad nigger is as good as another. More to the point, the articulation of these men's seductiveness had at its core a desire to return them to a Black American provincialism, if you will, the fact of a black singularity that was being daily challenged by the increased ability of Black American persons to live beyond the scope of their communities, a truth powerfully demonstrated by scores of black/white couples strolling down Fifth Avenue. Again Nikki Giovanni helps clarify my arguments:

> One day
> you gonna walk in this house
> and i'm gonna have on a long African gown
> you'll sit down and say "the Black . . ."
> and i'm gonna take an arm out
> then you—not noticing me at all—will say "what about
> this brother . . ."
> and i'm going to be slipping it over my head
> and you'll rapp on about "the revolution . . ."
> While i rest your hand against my stomach
> you'll go on—as you always do—saying
> "I just can't dig . . ."
> While i'm moving your hand up and down
> and i'll be taking your dashiki off
> then you'll say "What we really need . . ."
> and i'll be licking your arm
> and "the way I see it we ought to . . ."
> and unbuckling your pants
> "And what about the situation . . ."
> and taking your shorts off
> then you'll notice
> your state of undress
> and knowing you you'll just say

"Nikki,
isn't this counterrevolutionary . . .[15]

Giovanni's poem, aptly titled "Seduction," makes plain one of the main currents in black nationalist ideology. The model of black male masculinity she produces for us is most perfect, most radical, at precisely the moment at which it is naked, reduced to its original state, the savagery that her undressing reveals. Moreover, it is impossible to separate the allure of Giovanni's unnamed lover in this poem from the hot, bombastic, fully confrontational style that so captivated an entire generation of Americans. With one breath she asks if niggers can kill and with the next reveals a black seductiveness that is fueled by the same fiery rhetoric that would have us pissing on blond heads and driving '68 El Dorados over Protestants. When the word "Black" is spoken, an arm is revealed. When a brother is criticized, a woman disrobes. With talk of the revolution, hands begin to massage stomachs. With the statement of the people's need, an arm is licked; with the expression of radical vision, pants are unbuckled; a whiff of revolutionary analysis, and underwear fall to the floor.

Yet there is another, more insidious level on which seduction works within Giovanni's poetry. For even as the prize for the black male beloved is Giovanni's own body, this ultimately may prove to be a poor substitute for the radical consciousness and sense of engagement with the universal that is figured in contradistinction to an unproblematized black body. Giovanni asks, "Isn't this counterrevolutionary?" winking at her readers, suggesting that the black intellectualism so often on display during the heady days of the Black Power and Black Arts Movements might easily be overcome by an intense black sexual potency. Indeed once you go black you really never do go back.

I make these arguments with the awareness that a larger shift in American sexual mores operates as the backdrop for Giovanni's preoccupations. The postwar era was a moment in our country that witnessed a great coming out of increasingly vocal communities of sex radicals, including both interracialists and homosexuals. Indeed a white woman might appear, more or less unobstructed, with her black male lover precisely because the even more scandalous spectacle of the white woman with her black *female* lover was also becoming available to American communities. Thus we have a host of black chroniclers of the 1950s, 1960s, and 1970s: Amiri Baraka, Michele Wallace, Audre Lorde, James Baldwin, Malcolm X, Eldridge Cleaver, and Elaine Brown

herself commenting upon and oftentimes bemoaning the fact of the increased possibility for interracial sexual liaisons. Bull Connor be damned.[16]

At the same time, many, indeed most, of these writers were also concerned to point out the increased visibility of the urban homosexual. It becomes clear then that what is really being remarked is a sort of sexual substitution in which the homosexual might easily come to stand in for the interracialist.[17] The intense efforts to discipline so-called black desire such that
Black American people would come to narrate their pleasure taking in relation both to radical nationalist politics and to notions of an ancient African
corporeality existed cheek by jowl with equally intense efforts to demonstrate just how fake notions of normative—and profoundly racialized—
structures of desire actually were. Therefore the oft-noted disdain that many
nationalists had—and have—for homosexual persons and communities
ought to be read as a species of both sexual and racial panic. In "Of Liberation" Giovanni writes,

> Dykes of the world are united
> Faggots got their thing together
> (Everyone is organized)
> Black people these are the facts
> Where's your power[18]

Giovanni clearly understands that the reality of dykes uniting and faggots
getting their thing together is altogether indistinguishable from what one
imagines she believes to be the disillusionment of the Black American community, as evidenced by the increasingly apparent fact of the intimate asso-
ciations of black and white persons. All these presumably new forms of sexual affiliation, or rather the new boldness with which these forms were articulated, stemmed from a concerted effort to rescript the ontological status of
the body in American society such that it could no longer be counted on to
adhere to normative narratives of desire and affinity. The danger that confronts an essentially conservative writer like Giovanni then is that she will
be left out in the cold, adrift in a steadily changing sea of sexual/racial
mores in which even her old counterpart, the heterosexual black man,
might no longer be counted on for succor. Once one can no longer depend
on the comfort of a natural and ancient desire one is thrown back on one's
own improvised and highly contested attempts at pleasure. This means that
we must return to the ugliness of the here and now; we must acknowledge

the reality that erotic life takes place within contexts overburdened by the banality of racism and sexism.

> it's a sex object if you're pretty
> and no love
> or love and no sex if you're fat
> get back fat black woman be a mother
> grandmother strong thing but not woman
> gameswoman romantic woman love needer
> man seeker dick eater sweat getter
> fucking needing love seeking woman[19]

I hope that my readers will not take me as being too flippant when I say that Giovanni's remarkable expression of the racialized nature of sexual desire brings us directly back to the subject of Huey Newton's pussy. I have suggested that what the poems from which I have quoted reveal, even more potently than their author's revolutionary ardor, is the will to corral black sexuality or, more precisely, the modes of black seduction so apparent within American culture. Again what Giovanni posits here is that revolutionary desire is not undisciplined. On the contrary, the revolutionary enforces a narrative of desire that ultimately denies the reality of individuals involved in their blind pursuits of pleasure. Instead each amorous act becomes proof of black profundity. The lips touch Africa; the hands seek noble tradition. I would argue, therefore, that what Newton feared, as he climbed into and out of the beds of an adoring public, was that he would remain trapped within the frame of a potent, sexually vigorous, heterosexual black masculinity, a matrix by definition freighted with a number of quite apparent presuppositions about the essential provincialism of the subjects whom it encompassed that would ultimately prove to be suffocating or perhaps even deadly.

The scene that I presented above in which Newton and Brown pronounce upon the fact of Newton's seductiveness comes immediately prior to Newton's revealing to Brown that he anticipates the dismantling of the Black Panther Party and the production of a transracial, internationalist, anticapitalist movement in which he would no longer be revered as a Black American ultimate leader, radical saint. Newton had come through the crucible of nationalism and was preparing to help establish a vision of an American society that could see itself clear of the ugly strictures of race, class, and gender. One might argue, therefore, that, at least for a brief time, Newton attempted to refuse the intellectual trajectory suggested by Fanon, tried to reject a too-easy distinction between theoretical rigor and the ability to mobilize politically. He was particularly eager, therefore, at least with his most intimate confidante, to move beyond the fetishization of both his own life history and his own quite desirable body.

It is in this sense that I would ask us to reconsider Newton's often-repeated 1970 endorsement of the emerging gay-rights movement. His statement that "there is nothing to say that a homosexual cannot also be a revolutionary. . . . Quite the contrary, maybe a homosexual could be the most revolutionary"[20] consistently has been read as evidence in support of what many regard as an obvious truth and what others whisper as a tantalizing rumor. The truth is that Black American nationalist thought, as evidenced by Newton's speeches and writing, is much more modulated than many of its critics allow. Newton, Brown, George Jackson, Kathleen Cleaver, and a handful of other black nationalist intellectuals went to often-heroic lengths to understand and articulate the Black American liberation struggle in relation to international efforts against capitalist and imperialist domination as well as domestic efforts to secure personal liberties, most particularly control over one's own body. The rumor, one that persists to this day, was that Newton was gay, that his sensitivity to homosexual persons and movements was ultimately factored by desire for men and men's bodies.

What I would like to stress is that these two lines of thought, the factual and the subfactual, are part of the same discursive structure. They both continue to encourage the idea that there are real black bodies, identities, desires, and movements that necessarily precede performative, discursively framed bodies, identities, desires, and movements. Each continues, in fact, a species of triangulation by which students of black nationalism stand between competing versions of nationalist history and thought where, on the one hand, nationalists are read as provincial, conservative, and xenophobic, while, on the other hand, they are understood as cosmopolitan, progressive, and tolerant. It seems, in fact, that the critical literature surrounding black nationalism is almost obsessively concerned to demonstrate real black nationalists, beneath the patina of performance and political theater.[21] This is why so many of us continue to rework the trope of the clothed African savage in our efforts to create adequate narrative frameworks by which to understand the nationalist intellectuals whom we either celebrate or condemn. The tragedy of this mode of critical practice is that it cuts us off from deep consideration of the serious theoretical struggles undertaken by our most recent political and cultural ancestors and leaves us in the untenable position of having to create out of nothing, as it were, new political and theoretical bases for progressive community.

It is for just these reasons that I believe that Elaine Brown is almost compulsively concerned to present any number of multilayered scenes of triangulation within her autobiography. On the one hand, there is the triad produced by Brown, Newton, and Newton's somewhat self-effacing wife, Gwen Fountaine. The homoerotic charge between the two women is acted out upon the surface of Newton's body, producing him as a sort of living masthead, carved, naked breast prominently displayed in order to conceal the deep, messy trough of desire just below the surface. On the other hand, the two women begin, in Cuba, to appreciate one another, both preferring a living man to a dead martyr. It follows then that what the three achieve in Cuba is not simply a rapprochement but instead the disestablishment of the nationalist-inflected modes of heteronormativity that had come to dominate much of the party's thinking and practice. And perhaps more to the point, in that "third" location, Cuba, Newton, Brown, and Fountaine come to understand, however vaguely, just how simplistic notions regarding the intimate connection between current generations of Black Americans and long-dead Africans actually are. The ancient desire that they all presumably share pales in comparison with the creative pursuit of pleasure that they were promised. Newton for his part certainly wanted to move beyond a simpleminded articulation of a black potency and radicalism, predicated upon the notion of an African savagery unveiled, and toward the more complicated awareness that the Black American was not only modern but quintessentially American. He wanted, that is, to put his clothes back on.

Huey Newton, the Black Panther Party's Minister of Defense, was by all reports an almost pathologically shy man. It has also been reported that he was functionally illiterate. As a consequence, he needed, as almost any prominent performer might, disciplined functionaries—handlers, one might say—who could transcribe his speeches, answer his correspondence, keep the public at bay, and generally provide for his considerable needs. The day-to-day running of the party was eventually left to Brown, who would begin to so fear the cadre around Newton that she would flee the organization. Newton himself stopped making community appearances and never worked through his awkwardness with public speaking or his haphazard schooling. This was of course beside the point. His undoing, his doom, was that the image of Huey Newton had long since eclipsed the living reality of

Huey Newton. A moment arrived when Huey, the man, was no longer necessary in order to support the image of Huey, the "African" nationalist revolutionary, that has so successfully seduced generation after generation. As the titles of his two books, *Revolutionary Suicide* and *To Die for the People,* suggest, he was particularly aware that the rise of a heroic leader, a saint, necessitates the killing of an individual.[22]

Much of my work in *Once You Go Black* has been to suggest that (Black) Americans will never achieve the clean and noble connection to an ancient past for which so many of us long. We are not, it seems, ever quite saintly enough. We are, however, a profoundly modern, complex, and adaptable people. Indeed the difficult ontological and existential questions with which we must wrestle are precisely the questions to which much of the rest of the planet is only now awakening. Thus I am not so quick as many others are to try to explain away the political and ethical lapses of our leaders. I do not, for example, take the tragic final years of Newton's life, including his killing, as somehow distinct from his truly remarkable achievements as a younger man. Instead I understand that Black Americans, including the most talented among us, must improvise our existences. Thus our failures are just that, failures, and not, as is often said, evidence of either some innate inferiority *or* our having strayed too far from ancient paths.

I would propose then that we leave off with our attempts to read the real Huey Newton in relation to the performed Huey Newton. Instead I ask that we begin to understand and take seriously the fact that Newton attempted himself, especially during his time in Cuba, to move beyond this bifurcation of rhetoric and individuality, body and mind. I would argue that his willingness to address topics as seemingly out of character for a black nationalist leader as sexual liberation and gay rights acts itself as evidence of a will to break the hold that the logic of black historical and cultural profundity holds within the American imagination. Indeed he refuses altogether the split between the revolutionary theorist coolly delivering his thesis on the people's liberation and the bad, black radical lover, hotly satisfying his partner's desire.

I will close by reiterating a point that I made early in this chapter. Those of us most concerned with questions of identity, including those of us who carry the name "queer," do not serve our interests as well as we might by maintaining an aloof, dismissive posture to our own political and intellectual genealogies. I have taken as long as I have to explicate some of the complicated structure of Black American nationalist thought not simply as a means by which to decry a lack of progressive critique of gender and sexuality within black nationalism nor even to bemoan the passing of those wonderful years within American radicalism dominated by beautiful black persons sporting breathtakingly large Afros but instead to take partial account of the forms of intellectualism and leadership available to Black Americans, and all Americans, during those years and beyond and the rather exacting price that we have had to pay for the articulation of those forms. The contemporary history of the Black American might be properly rendered, in fact, as the rising of great leaders, their rather well-anticipated deaths, and our continued mourning for their lost potential. Martin Luther King, Malcolm X, Medgar Evers, George Jackson, Huey Newton, all dead, all remembered. I must hasten to say that I am not certain that it is at all possible to separate the fact of these men's untimely deaths—and timeless innocence—from the reality that they continue to maintain such a powerful hold on the American national imagination. What is certain, however, is that we must insist upon a new level of maturity in our production of politics and culture. We must give up on the idea that there can be either innocent communities or innocent leaders. In doing so, I would suggest that a first important step might be to remove ourselves from the position of having either to defend or condemn our all-too-sullied recent past.

5

Queer Sweetback

Just as masculinity always constructs femininity as double—simultaneously Madonna and Whore—so racism constructs the black subject: noble savage and violent avenger. And in the doubling, fear and desire double for one another and play across the structures of otherness, complicating in politics.

—Stuart Hall, "New Ethnicities"

Sire, these lines are not an homage to brutality that the artist has invented, but a hymn from the mouth of reality.

—traditional prologue of the Middle Ages

I begin with a question: What sort of moment is this in which to pose the question of a queer black studies? Moreover, in posing this question one must immediately repeat the now fundamental observation that these moments are always conjunctural, that they have their historical specificity; and although they always exhibit similarities and continuities with the other moments in which we pose a question like this, they are never the same moment. I want to speak then in the simplest terms possible about the particular challenges faced by American intellectuals, especially those of us concerned with confluences of race, class, gender, and sexuality, as we attempt not only to map what we are certain has passed already (the varied stories of our various becomings) but also and more importantly where exactly we seem to have arrived. The task is made more difficult still when the intellectual recognizes, presumably with some humility, that he exists neither at the beginning nor the end of any historical trajectory but always at the dynamic, if never wholly articulate, center. One might rightly claim then that it is a historical peculiarity that the revolutionary intellectual ever fully understands the profundity of his revolt, as the apparatuses at his disposal, his most efficacious methods of effecting change, are inevitably those with which his society effects its own reproduction. Thus I will follow, with as much precision as possible, the many clues given us by cultural critic

Stuart Hall in his several celebrated attempts to explain the nature of the historical shifts that allowed for the articulation of a so-called black popular culture. That is to say, I understand that the notion of a Queer Black Studies is itself evidence of a historical shift in which European high culture has presumably been eclipsed by the banalities of the American popular, and in which the realities of the "global postmodern" seem to foster an environment in which old distinctions between center and periphery are forcefully rearticulated within politics even as they are increasingly read as meaningless within culture. More to the point, I will attempt to hew as closely as I can to the simple recognition that it is not nearly so easy as presumably it once was to establish with anything approaching certainty the essence of either a queer or a black subjectivity.

It is for these reasons that one cannot, or at least *should not,* continue the laughable ritual of declaiming, on the one hand, the emptiness of race and sexuality as modes of signification while, on the other, maintaining that even so, one certainly "knows one when one sees one." Or to pick up the rhetoric of at least a half dozen of my interlocutors, I do not concede that no matter the precision with which one makes one's claims about the instability of rhetorics of race, class, sexuality, and gender that this logic is always eclipsed by the ready knowledge of the steely eyed policeman presumably waiting just outside the lecture-hall doors. Indeed I continue to take a certain intellectual and ethical obstinacy to be absolutely necessary in our efforts to wean ourselves from the most disturbing aspects of American and European racialisms. In particular, I reject out of hand comfortable notions regarding the Black American's essential and abiding innocence in relation to what one might think of as the underbelly of modern society. Slavery, the Holocaust, imperial wars, colonialism, neocolonialism, terror and terrorism all come readily to mind. I do so, moreover, precisely because, as Hall suggests above and as I have argued throughout *Once You Go Black,* this notion is but one side of the same grubby ideological coin on which also is printed the monstrous face of the black brute. It is my intention, therefore, to engage my critics on their own ground. Thus I will supplement my initial query, "What sort of moment is this in which to pose the question of a queer black studies?" with a second that I hope may help us in our efforts at cobbling together an answer to the first: Why in responding to the claim that Black American persons are, in fact, agents of history and, moreover, that we have chosen (in however limited a manner one wishes to use that term) the very modes with which we address questions of difference do critics inevitably return to a sort of metaphysics of difference in which Black Americans are refigured as animated objects, noble victims, the vaguely discernible subaltern, the never fully articulate other?

In Chicago make a claim about the innate freedom of all persons, black or otherwise, and you will most certainly be met with the clumsy, grumpy response, "Ah yes, that may be true here, but certainly one cannot say such things on the south side." Repeat one's claims in New York, and logic seems to unravel as one heads further north. In Baltimore and Berlin the questionable direction is east. And always, one is reminded of that never present but always lurking policeman who, presumably having read Althusser with great precision, will call out, immediately upon encountering a brown-skinned man, aged fifteen to fifty, with hair arranged in curls or kinks, "Hey you there!" I must say, however, that in the American context one of the most potent markers of the historical shift that I am attempting to remark is that the proper response to such a hail may not be, "Yes I am, in fact, black," or to continue in the spirit of my initial comments, "I am indeed both black and queer," but instead simply, "Yes, Mister Secretary. You called?" or more disturbing still, "No Madame Director. The weapons have yet to be discovered."[1] Of course, it is not my intention to deny the rather vicious methods of policing (of which the uniformed officer is but the most basic manifestation) by which immigrants, women, poor persons, racial and sexual minorities have been and are manipulated and exploited in both the United States and Europe. Instead I would suggest that this tendency on the part of American cultural critics in particular and Western critics in general to overprivilege the policeman's hail is itself evidence of what Hall describes as a " 'nothing ever changes, the system always wins' attitude," which operates as a protective shell that prevents even the most able of critics from "developing cultural strategies that can make a difference."[2] And as I will argue below, the primacy of this particular model of subjectivity and subjectification is itself indicative of American ideologies of race that remain coherent precisely because they are imagined as timeless and unchanging.

I must ask your forbearance then as I allow full range to some of my more perverse intellectual proclivities and turn, as it were, to our spectral man-at-arms and attempt to listen for a moment or two to what he has to say. For indeed Althusser's articulation of the policeman's hail is clearly itself an attempt to reconfigure Hegel's model of the struggle between master and slave as perhaps *the* primary form of what we have come to think of as the discursive. My only addition in these pages has been to point out the obvious fact that in both iterations, even in the absence of ready evidence, one presumes the interlocutors to be men, most often of the black and white varieties. Indeed the clumsy philosophical maxim cum American common sense that I noted in the introduction, "The master strikes the slave, the slave strikes back, and thus a man is created," continues with an uncanny precision not so much in Althusser's theses regarding hegemony and interpellation as in our own often too heavy-handed rearticulations of the same: The policeman yells "nigger," the nigger responds "pig," and thus racial distinction continues forever and anon. The problem of course is that the workings of the hegemonic are never quite as pretty as all that. Indeed, as I have said, part of the deep structure of the rhetoric here is the assumption that what we are discussing is the white *male* policeman's hailing of the black *male* subject. Though it is well within the range of the commonsensical to assume that white men call blacks into being, any more complicated configuration than this is all but preposterous. The gruffly rendered, "Hey you there!" can almost never be answered satisfactorily with the sentence, "Yes, I am, in fact, white and heterosexual, educated and propertied." For, as we know already, part of the manner in which the hegemonic functions is that certain dominant social positions are all too infrequently announced, at least, that is to say, not in anything approaching polite company.

Surely you have recognized that part of what I am attempting is to note again the homoeroticism embedded within what can arguably be said to be *the* most productive philosophical model available to scholars of Black American history and culture. At this late hour it is, in fact, among the easiest of procedures to point out the ways in which the basic structures of modernity, most particularly race and class, have been and are conceptualized as precisely struggles between men. This does not mean, however, that what I am after is a simple unveiling of ancient homoerotics or antique homosexualities. Though I have promised a discussion of the means by which a Queer Black Studies might announce itself, I must leave the question of a queer black subjectivity bracketed. We are not engaged in a process of historical recovery. We shall not, indeed we cannot, go back and get "it," as I am frightfully confused as to what that "it" actually entails. We can, however, look more closely into the theoretical models by which we define racial and sexual difference. We can pay much more precise attention to the stakes involved in the all-but-constant rearticulation of these models and the ways in which these articulations have been precisely structured to leave unstated obvious realities about race, class, gender, and sex as they are actually lived and experienced in America. While masters and slaves, policemen and nig-gers have undoubtedly struggled with fists and weapons, they have even more assuredly struggled with mouths and lips, buttocks and breasts, vagi-nas and penises, pretty smiles and lovely hair, not to mention all the detri-tus, both the high and the low, of modern civilization. I would argue, more-over, that my ability to state this matter with at least a modicum of clarity and even my ability to place not only Hegel and Althusser but also Masters and Slaves, Policemen and Niggers in a ledger marked "Queer" suggests his-torical and conceptual change that if not profound is at the very least pro-vocative.

It seems then that the rules of the game have changed. For we are no longer concerned with the matter of who can speak for the queer black but instead with the ways in which the most basic conceits of American culture turn on the messy connection between the erotic and the coercive, the po-liceman's heavy-handed violence and the subtle, or not so subtle, manipula-tion of that same policeman's desire. I will take a risk then and reach beyond myself to make a claim about the present that will be necessarily flawed, as I too am embedded in this moment, writing at a great mahogany desk, on a dull rainy afternoon in another borrowed apartment at the center of yet an-other war-scarred European capital. Thin shards of yellow and gray litter the afternoon sky. Chimes ring lightly. Smoke drifts up lazily from a cigarette, reminding one of the guilt inevitably attached to even the most common American pleasures. I say these things, attach lovely words to even more lovely objects and moments as a preface to my announcement that I do be-lieve that the violence that has been visited upon my country and the much more profound violence that my country has visited on many others do have a quite specific import for American intellectuals who would mark themselves as either black or queer. There is no way in which any one of us can claim innocence, no manner in which we might carefully disimbricate our earnest work from the realities of war, torture, deprivation, or occupa-tion. Though these lovely rooms are not splattered in blood, though no child's screams mar the carefully tuned ringing of chimes, these things have come, in fact, at an almost unfathomably high price.

What sort of moment is this in which to pose the question of a queer black studies? It is a moment in which even the least careful observer might recognize that any endeavor that is dependent upon the largess of the grand institutions of the United States and Europe (and both queer and black stud-ies certainly merit inclusion on this list) operates somewhere in that tight, difficult space created by the struggles of masters with slaves, policemen with niggers, soldiers with captives. Or to be more precise, the rhetorics that we utilize to describe the problematics of American subjectivity remain incredibly limited, turning as they do on the logic of a never-ending, never-changing struggle between dominant and submissive, top and bottom, that increasingly loses utility precisely because so few critics have been willing or able to read the obvious erotic codes embedded therein. Thus though I must reiterate the correctness of Virginia Woolf's claims that the modern intellectual cannot reproduce himself in the absence of quiet rooms, a few extra guineas, leisure, and perhaps even the furtively consumed cigarette, indeed that it may be impossible to distinguish him from these, his most precious, possessions, I do understand that all of these things are secured for us, in our name, as it were, with bullets and cuffs, the inventions and interventions of clever soldiers and most importantly that heavy-rolling gait and steely gaze of the man-at-arms. Indeed the notion of the intellectual, innocently at work in his study: mahogany desk, well-tuned chimes, shards of pink and gray, is itself dependent upon ideas about how subjectivity is fashioned that would forever counterpoise the quiet contemplation of the study with the raucous grind of the street.

I must be careful, therefore, not to let myself sink too deeply into the comfort of my own pessimism. For though the news from home continues on a downward spiral from not good to bad to worse, I remain aware that this news is not in fact the sum total of who we are. I understand that the hegemonic works in both directions, from top to bottom, bottom to top. Indeed one of the primary challenges for the committed American intellectual at this historical juncture is precisely to embrace the fact of his culpability, the fact of his connection to the rest of his community, and in so doing to allow for a better understanding of the ways in which the potency of America's fascination with its own presumed innocence has become part and parcel of the many apparatuses with which our country justifies and enacts its dominance and violence. For the black intellectual, the queer intellectual, or the black and queer intellectual the specific challenge is to understand that the time has long since passed when one might innocently disavow one's connection to one's nation. The time is ripe for us to move beyond the simple arithmetic procedure of insisting that one can be black and gay and an intellectual and an American and toward consideration of the fact that these distinctions may ultimately be less significant than we had imagined. We must remain constantly aware that we are defeated at the outset if we

continue to allow the idea that American innocence always comes beautifully wrapped in packages of brown and black, yellow and red, or even the
more showy lavender and pink.

I

certain ways in which black men continue to live out their counter-iden-
tities as black masculinities and replay those fantasies in the theatres of
popular culture are, when viewed from along other axes, the very masculine identities that are oppressive to women, that claim visibility for
their hardness only at the expense of the vulnerability and feminization
of gay black men. The way in which a transgressive politics in one do-
main is constantly sutured and stabilized by unexamined politics in another is only to be explained by the continuous cross-dislocation of one
identity by another, one structure by another. Dominant ethnicities are
always underpinned by a particular sexual economy, a particular figured
masculinity, a particular class identity.
—Stuart Hall, "What Is This 'Black' in Black Popular Culture?"

Where you get that *we* shit?
—Melvin Van Peebles, *Sweet Sweetback's Baadasssss Song*

Melvin Van Peebles, writer, director, novelist, composer, and provocateur,
became something of a cult icon in 1971 with the release of his classic feature, *Sweet Sweetback's Baadasssss Song*. It was not just that this *very* low-
budget independent managed to earn some ten million dollars in box-office
receipts, becoming in the process one of the highest grossing independent
films of the year. Nor was it that the work was seen (correctly I believe) as the
first in a long line of so-called Blaxploitation features, whose revenues were
largely responsible for salvaging the financial prospects of a sluggish American film industry. Instead Van Peebles, whose own compelling life story has
now been committed to celluloid via the efforts of his son, Mario, became
such a significant voice within 1970s (Black) American cultural life precisely
because he was understood to be one of the first artists to bring not only
compelling but realistic images of Black Americans into mainstream cine-
mas, breaking with decades-long traditions in which blacks were portrayed
as either shockingly servile (Butterfly McQueen), impossibly honorable (Sid-

ney Poitier), or perhaps not black at all (Susan Kohner in Douglas Sirk's 1959 classic, *Imitation of Life*).

Van Peebles is rather meticulous, in fact, in his efforts to disestablish the great dividing line between audience and screen, not only giving place of honor in the credits to "The Black Community" and "Brer Soul" but also utilizing the considerable talents of the then largely unknown funk group "Earth, Wind and Fire," as well as liberally seasoning the film with "found" footage of black persons and communities in and around Los Angeles. Of course part of what I am attempting is to remark the new level of self-consciousness on display among Black American intellectuals of the 1960s and 1970s, a self-consciousness altogether suited to the medium of film. As I suggested in the last chapter, one of the most significant responses of midcentury black intellectuals to the ethical ambiguity that was the legacy left by Wright, Ellison, and Baldwin, among others, was to embrace exactly the racialist visual vocabulary first identified by Frantz Fanon. That is to say, by focusing on image and style, artists like Van Peebles hoped to settle the difficult questions surrounding Black American identity by resuscitating the very naive connections between the visual, the ontological, and the epistemological ("I know one when I see one") that an entire generation of cultural workers had been at pains to disrupt.

Thus *Sweet Sweetback*'s significance goes far beyond its status as the first work within a new genre. Instead what *Sweet Sweetback* accomplishes is the rearticulation of a grammar of Black American realism (ghetto violence, grinding poverty, confrontations with police and state, and most especially a certain potent and almost inexhaustible black sexuality) that continues today as a primary discursive mode (with perhaps even more vigor) in the efforts of a host of hip-hop artists, all of whom, strangely enough, seem to hail from exactly six communities in New York, California, and a nebulous South/West/Midwest conglomeration. We can see quite clearly then why Van Peebles might open his work with the epigram translated from the French with which I began this chapter, "Sire, these lines are not an homage to brutality that the artist has invented, but a hymn from the mouth of reality," as the film's very syntax is dependent upon the conceit that there is no essential disconnect between the performers on screen and the real lives they perform. Instead the film might be said to be outfitting itself with a sort of hyperrealism, a vigorous, bare-bones truth-telling about the realities of Black America that would *not* be possible within more effete art forms. And to give Van Peebles his due, one of the ways that he succeeds in *Sweet Sweetback* is to eschew the linear and cumulative modes of storytelling most commonly available in the modern novel for an imagistic and, I would say, static aesthetic that focuses less on story than on mood, moment, and most importantly style.

Again I turn to the work of Stuart Hall to help clarify my thinking on these matters. For it was Hall who most forcefully and most succinctly articulated the decided shift in Black American popular cultural production away from the narratological and toward the stylistic, suggesting that "within the black repertoire, *style*—which mainstream cultural critics often believe to be the mere husk, the wrapping, the sugar-coating on the pill—has become *itself* the subject of what is going on." He continues by pointing out that this emphasis on husks, wrappings, and sugar-coats has had the effect of undermining the centrality of fiction and criticism within (Black) American conceptions of cultural sophistication, with the result being that we see artists relying in an ever more heavy-handed manner on the so-called black body in their ongoing efforts to figure the varied politics of black cultural representation.[3]

I would add that one of the most obvious yet least stated realities of the Blaxploitation phenomenon that Van Peebles helped initiate is that it speaks directly to the fact that at midcentury the Black American no longer possessed what one might call the "material factuality" that he once had. That is to say, the transition from Negro to Black involved not only movement from south to north, country to city, farm to factory but also and no less spectacularly from a seemingly well-established ontological certainty to a necessarily unsettling ideological and epistemological instability. Moreover, as I have argued throughout *Once You Go Black,* the most historically significant consequence of the mass transformations in technologies of travel and communication (train and telephone, airplane and Internet) witnessed by twentieth-century Americans may not be the breathtaking accumulations of wealth, poverty, violence, labor, and leisure with which we are all too familiar but instead the radical reconfiguration of the body (and the presumed difference inscribed on it) that has, in fact, been a primary tool in the production and reproduction of these always overfull stockpiles. As the so-called black body becomes an ever more abstract entity it can be burdened with ever more complicated and abstracted labors. Thus one might rightly define Blaxploitation as yet another articulation of that extremely rigorous discipline within filmic practice in which "race" is always figured not only as substantial but timeless, in which blackness might be understood to exist not only in field and factory but also in apartments, studios, and on screens to boot. This is why in the practice of this phony discipline, in this constant reiteration of the naive ideological maxim that film does not *produce* racial difference but only *represents* it, the most potent weapon in the hands of the ideologue is, as Hall suggests, the (black) body.

Recognizing this might help us to understand just why Van Peebles and his director of photography, Bob Maxwell, spend so much time focused on the lush textures of Black American flesh. The opening sequence of *Sweet Sweetback* includes a series of close shots of the faces of women—black, yellow, red, brown, smiling, pensive, sad, and bored—who watch as a frighteningly disheveled young boy, played by an adolescent Mario Van Peebles, eats with relish the stew that a particularly buxom woman continuously spoons onto his plate. This is followed by a scene in which we see one of the women cleaning herself in a small room in what we now understand is a house of prostitution, as the young boy—clothes, hair, and skin all in good form—walks past to deliver towels outside one of the house's many doors. The prostitute invites the boy into her room, and in a scene that has become one of the most controversial in the history of Black American cinema, she disrobes, instructs the boy to do the same, and initiates him into manhood, as it were, making a direct connection between the feeding of the stomach with stew and the feeding of the loins with this woman's deliciously hot body. In the course of their encounter, gospel music begins to play in the background, and the prostitute, seasoned though she may be, loses herself in the moment and begins to scream in ecstasy as the young boy grinds above her. "You got a sweet, sweetback," she tells him, and a character, if not a star, is born.

Of course we see succinctly stated almost every stereotype of Black American life: poverty, criminality, precocious sexuality, an absence of proper familial structure, not to mention high levels of religiosity and a penchant for rich foods. Even so, I must rush to say that my goal here is not to criticize Van Peebles for wallowing in the deep muck of American racialism. On the contrary, it is not difficult for me to understand how American audiences accustomed to a steady diet of black characters who lacked any sort of sexual assertiveness would find both Van Peebles's frankness and his funkiness compelling. It is worth noting in this regard that the scene is provocative not simply because of its depiction of nonromantic, intergenerational sex but also because Van Peebles and Maxwell are so relentless in their use of the camera to reassure the audience that they are, in fact, watching real black persons engaged in very real sexual acts.[4] The camera is never placed more than a few feet away from the two actors as it continually serves up Van Peebles's own peculiarly erotic stew of close shots. The woman's lips, legs, thighs, hips, the boy's buttocks, arms, back, and even more significantly his penis and her rather unruly hair, are all examined in intimate detail. That is to say, Van Peebles, who experiments throughout the film with lighting techniques that previously had been thought of as mistakes, is eager in these scenes to scrub *Sweet Sweetback* clean of that glossy, polished look that had come to so typify Hollywood directors and to so bore American audiences. Or as Van Peebles has been careful to state at every available opportunity, this was not a Hollywood film but one with an amateur cast and crew whose primary goal was the expression of that indefinable but always palpable entity, soul.

The difficulty is that all the gospel music, bad lighting, and nappy hair in the world could never change the reality that what Van Peebles did, in fact, produce, what indeed I am now responding to, was not soul per se (a thing that like any metaphysics one might affirm or deny but never truly explicate) but film. Moreover, one of the more intriguing aspects of Van Peebles's intellect is that though he produced a work designed to obscure all evidence of its own production, he nonetheless remained aware (presumably as lights were hoisted above his head and actors were primped if not coiffed) that film is an even more impersonal, technologically driven, and capital-dependent medium than is fiction. Moreover, the audience member, sitting in front of the movie screen, the video monitor, or, worse yet, the computer can never fully forget the technological feats that he is witnessing. This is true even and especially as he winces at the incongruity of a young boy laboring above a woman's body as a choir sings the spiritual "Wade in the Water."

We can see, therefore, why Van Peebles hiccups, as it were, in this profoundly "soulful" scene, giving to the young actress working with his son the impossibly incongruous lines, "You ain't at the photographer's. You ain't getting your picture taken. Move!" One might very easily make the observation that a more self-conscious bit of dialogue had not been heard in American cinema since Dorothy and her friends were told to never mind the furtive activities of that strange fellow behind the curtains. Indeed it seems almost that Van Peebles is daring his audience to recognize the joke, the high-stakes irony, inherent in an actress in moving pictures telling her on-screen counterpart to move as his picture is *not* being taken. The device that Van Peebles utilizes here is not indistinct from that of the magician who confuses and mystifies his audience precisely through the deployment of gestures so broad that one more often than not misses what is passing right before one's eyes. And as if the gesture were not already broad enough, Van Peebles supplements it with one of the most provocative moments of editing in American cinematography. The camera closes in on the prostitute caught up in her ecstasy as the young Van Peebles flops and fumbles. When he finishes, however, and as the camera pulls back we see that the young boy has developed into a man, the adult Sweetback, an individual who we now see has never left the house of prostitution but has, in fact, become one of the main attractions in the sex shows that the house's owner, Beetle, regularly stages.

I think it important that we pause for a moment to consider the importance of the ideological work that Van Peebles accomplishes with these several simple gestures. It is not just that the adult Sweetback, played by Melvin, is obviously meant to be taken as *the* child (the soul, some might say) of a community. Nor is it even that this soulfulness is understood to exist precisely on the margins of black society, in a house that is most certainly *not* a home. Instead I would argue that part of what Van Pebbles achieves is a negation of the very idea of historical progression that was so central a component in the ideological arsenal of the generation of black intellectuals that preceded him. In this scene what is discarded is the classic device of representing the development of the Black American community (from slavery to freedom, if you will) via the story of the young boy cum successful adult. (Recall Richard Wright's preoccupation with Mississippi.) In so doing, Van Peebles seriously undermines a traditional politics of representation in which the inevitable advancement of the black community was thought to be as self-evident as the inevitable development of the (black) child.

In *Sweet Sweetback*, however, surprisingly little advancement, development, or what have you actually takes place. Indeed what little narrative progression we do see occurs only when Sweetback is loaned by Beetle, after a performance that I will discuss in greater depth below, to two white police officers who want to make a show of diligence by bringing in a suspect for the recent murder of a black Angelino. While executing this "eyewash," they are called to disrupt a protest being led by a minor character, Mumu, whom they do not formally arrest but instead take to a secluded area to torture. Sweetback, in a moment of valor that is never fully explained, defends

157

Mumu, using the policemen's own cuffs as his weapon, miraculously subduing both officers. Mumu, now free, faces his savior and asks, "Where we going?" Sweetback, just about to begin the process of running and deception that will make up the majority of the film, answers with precision, "Where you get that *we* shit?"

It should be clear by now that I intend to demonstrate some of the very simple ways in which Van Peebles redirects the attention of his audiences away from the reality that what they are seeing on screen is not "The Black Community" or "Brer Soul" but instead a group of actors (amateurs though they may be) whose work is supported by an even larger group of technicians and stylists. That said, I would remind you that I am also concerned with a set of ethical and philosophical questions to which I believe Van Peebles's practice alerts us. If Stuart Hall is correct (and I believe he is) that we are at the end of the era of black innocence, then I think that it makes sense for us to try to map the historical trajectory of this particular moment in Black American cultural history as best we can.

Moreover, I hope it is patently obvious by this point that my negative interest in the trope of Black American innocence is but one more tool in my ongoing efforts to question notions of a profound, ahistorical, and unchanging black tradition which none of us can either escape or affect. Thus I must ask when exactly did *innocence* become a significant term in the varied politics of Black American cultural representation? My supposition (and again I remind you that I am as much at the center of this moment as are you) is that we would be best served by *not* following in the well-worn paths that lead from the sufferings of the enslaved up to the half-realized jubilations of today. We should not continue with the logic in which there is no distinction between the enslaved body and the body that now participates in the writing of these lines. Or to state the matter in a less obtuse manner, while there is a great deal one might celebrate about Van Peebles, the filmmaker, one would be hard-pressed to describe the positive attributes of Van Peebles, the historian.

On the contrary, what Van Peebles accomplishes in *Sweet Sweetback* is a bold articulation of the *contemporary* American notion that our country *has not* advanced beyond the world of meaning and affect produced during our centuries-long sojourn in and with slavery. Thus for Van Peebles there is no essential disconnect between the struggles of Black American citizens during the mid-twentieth century and the desperate flights of enslaved black persons during the mid-nineteenth. The many scenes of Sweetback's running

through a Los Angeles landscape that morphs miraculously into a depopu-
lated, only partially industrialized countryside, abetted by the unfortunate
device of tracking dogs, clearly work to paint Sweetback as exactly the same
type of fugitive, pursued for exactly the same reasons, as were, say, Frederick Douglass and William Wells Brown, Harriet Tubman, William and Ellen
Craft. And in so doing, in suggesting that the innocence of the fugitive is
one and the same with the innocence of the modern pornographer, what
Van Peebles and those many intellectuals whom I take him to represent do is
evacuate the term *innocence* of any usefulness, any meaning in the modern
world of politics and culture. For my part I believe that the so-called innocence that is under assault today is by definition a contemporary phenomenon, an ideological reconfiguration of Black American subjectivity that has
its roots precisely in that moment in history, roughly the thirty years or so
following World War II, when the Black American community, besieged as it
was, was no longer wholly overdetermined by either condition of servitude,
caste, region, or more importantly for our efforts here, the clumsiness of
more ancient forms of representation such as the book.

I think it would be useful for me to remind my readers of the arguments
that I made in the previous chapter regarding "the clothed African savage"
and most particularly the ways in which midcentury Black American intellectuals put this notion to quite productive use. Thus I will refer you again to
Norman Mailer's infamous 1957 thesis on white Negroes and his insistence
that as the bad black is cultureless, alienated, psychopathic, hated from
within and without, he is necessarily physically healthy and "spiritually" innocent.[5] Thus for Mailer, writing at midcentury and taking the jazz musician
as his model, the salvation of a sluggish, technologically dependent, culturally and ethically bankrupt nation will necessarily be effected by precisely
that part of the population that finds itself least ensnared within the traps of
modern civilization. It is, therefore, through the asociality of the jazz man
and the many white Negroes who emulate him that the innocence of a lost
America can be nourished and eventually resurrected. Of course, it was not
the domesticated Negro, the so-called Uncle Tom, on whom Mailer pinned
his hopes for the renewal of American culture, aesthetics, and ethics but, on
the contrary, the Negro in revolt, the violent avenger, to quote Hall, who
with his trumpet, saxophone, and dick, if not his sword, shield, and gun,
will deliver our great country from its even greater wickedness.

I intend to read Van Peebles alongside Mailer, to situate the two artists
within the same historical moment and to charge black Van Peebles with

the same primitivism that I believe was rightly ascribed to white Mailer. My critique of Van Peebles, however, is not so much that like Mailer he places his hopes for a nation and a people on an antisocial character, Sweetback, who is a sex worker, a criminal, an orphan, and who to make matters worse, rarely speaks (Van Peebles claims he has only six lines). Instead, I would suggest to you that Van Peebles's great error is that he has set about announcing a black character without subjectivity. Indeed it is precisely my fear and distaste for this phenomenon, this vacant blackness, that has led me to criticize repeatedly our tendency to frame all discussions of black intellectual life within outmoded conceptions of a static Black American history and culture. In Van Peebles's drive to graphically represent the soul of Black America he produces a Sweetback who, like Ellison's character Rhinehart in *Invisible Man,* is so very *a*social that he exists for neither whites *nor* blacks. His blackness is so intense, so all-encompassing, so very dark that he ultimately cannot be seen by the very community that he purportedly represents.

It is in this sense that I would argue that Sweetback exists outside history, whether one names this history "white" *or* "black." One of the most profound aspects of the film, in fact, is its continual reframing of the faces of black persons who, standing squarely in front of the camera, state again and again that they have not seen Sweetback, as indeed they have not and as they cannot, for Sweetback represents such a pure fantasy of blackness (the outraged, running Negro who exists wholly outside the social) that he becomes less a man than a specter, a dream, a ghost operating decidedly outside the machine. His meager lines, delivered at moments of extreme crisis ("Where you get that *we* shit?" "I want you to cover for me," "I'm going upstairs to the farm," "Fucking," "Take Him," "He's Our Future Bruh"), never produce any more depth within his character. Instead they are almost always utilized as a means by which to keep Sweetback running, as it were, to disallow any connection to family, home, community, or nation and to cast him as that "Baad Asss Nigger Coming to Collect Some Dues" for whom oppressive whites and complicit blacks should "watch out!"

Still, there is the matter of that "hiccupping" within Van Peebles's artistic practice that I attempted to describe previously. There is a sense that one gets while watching *Sweet Sweetback* that its director was much more sensitive than Mailer ever was to the ways in which both the Black American artist and the Black American folk hero are subjects who have been worked on from within and from without, who could gain no substance in the absence of community, both the black and the white, and culture, both the high and the low. Stuart Hall writes of this matter,

> The point of underlying over-determination—black cultural repertoires constituted from two directions at once—is perhaps more subversive than you think. It is to insist that in black popular culture, strictly speaking, ethnographically speaking, there are no pure forms at all. Always these forms are the product of partial synchronization, of engagement across cultural boundaries, of the confluence of more than one cultural tradition, of the negotiations of dominant and subordinate positions, of the subterranean strategies of recoding and transcoding, of critical signification, of signifying.[6]

In the particular case of *Sweet Sweetback* I want to suggest not only that Van Peebles recognizes the ways in which even the blackest of Black American cultural forms are established through processes of synchronization, hybridization, negotiation, and engagement across boundaries, a point that frankly it seems to me any clever Black American eleven-year-old ought to be able to master without breaking a sweat, but also that part of what is so fascinating about Van Peebles is that he plays with this hybridization within Black America in a manner that ultimately works to rearticulate the very economy of innocence and historical profundity that I have been attempting to demonstrate throughout *Once You Go Black*. Indeed though Van Peebles brings our attention back to the reproductive and sexual connotations embedded within the word *hybrid* (body to body, belly to belly), he does so not as a testament to the ultimately impure reality that is Black America but instead to remind his audience of their already well-established ideas regarding the Black American's potent sexuality which opens out onto a sort of natural cosmopolitanism. Or to utilize some of the vernacular of Van Peebles's moment, the fact the we are a people who are hot sexually (read adventurous, insatiable, funky, ever ready) is precisely that which makes us cool in almost all other endeavors.

It is this savory mix of the sexually potent with the cosmopolitan, unrelenting heat with unfathomable coolness, that Van Peebles attempts to demonstrate in the sequence immediately following Sweetback's sexual initiation. This scene, aptly titled "Performance Art," opens with more close shots. This time, however, they are of an interracial crowd of men and women who have arrived at Beetle's house to view one of the sex spectacles for which the place is famous. From off screen one of the prostitutes enters, dressed in a white mini and carrying a bouquet of flowers. We of course are meant to recognize her as a sexual novice ready for the taking at the hands of one of Southern California's many sweetbacks. Suddenly another character appears on the scene. Dressed in a man's suit and wearing an obviously false beard, this second entrant into the spectacle wastes no time pursuing the young vixen, grabbing her roughly, pressing against her body, pushing her to the ground, then disrobing and bidding her to do the same in a manner that rather self-consciously maps the scene before with Sweetback. The twist is that, surprise surprise, the "man" who one presumes has just accosted a young girl turns out to be a woman, as demonstrated not only by the tight brassiere she wears beneath her man's suit but also by the large dildo that she wears strapped between her legs. This in no way hinders the show, however, as soul music is piped in from the background, and the one woman repeatedly enters the other with her "false penis" on the floor of the makeshift theater. Finally, the butch woman, still wearing her bra and beard but her dildo nowhere in sight, disengages from her lover, gets on her knees, and places her hands in front of her face in a position of prayer. The music stops. The screen goes black. The crowd ceases its raucous banter. We enter a moment of low-budget sex-club serenity which is not broken until a flaming sparkler, the type carried by children at Fourth of July celebrations, is lit.

This time, however, the fire, the single light in this particular well of loneliness, is carried by a transvestite dressed in the wings and robes of a fairy. She says, as the crowd cackles and guffaws, "I am the Good Dyke Fairy Godmother. Didn't you know that all good dykes have fairy godmothers? And I'm here to answer the prayers of a good dyke. Zap child." With that, the butch woman removes her bra and beard, and through the magic of amateur editing it is revealed that the woman has changed into a man, indeed into Sweetback himself. It is at this point that this clever scene goes the way of almost all heterosexual pornography. The real man enacts the procedures of which the butch lesbian, with her strapped-on masculinity, has dreamed. Again the screen is filled with legs and buttocks, lips and that telltale unkempt hair until finally the woman screams in ecstasy and Sweetback is praised and caressed by the Good Dyke Fairy Godmother in the same manner in which one would treat a prize stallion or steer after a successful mating.

One might still rightfully claim that even with all the clichés that this particular passage rehearses it is nonetheless refreshing in the ways it makes apparent the manner in which heterosexual sexual practice (one is almost tempted to say the spectacle of heterosexuality) is always framed by butch dykes, precocious young girls, not to mention Good Dyke Fairy Godmothers. Indeed this was precisely what I was attempting to get at earlier when I argued that Van Peebles recognizes the ways in which even the blackest of Black American cultural forms are established through processes of synchronization, hybridization, negotiation, and engagement across boundaries. Moreover, if there is a clearer manner by which to demonstrate the sexual connotations of the word *hybrid,* I am at a loss to do so at this juncture. I would submit to you, however, that though this scene actively flaunts a sort of sexual/racial/cultural sophistication, it does so precisely as a means by which to reiterate, indeed to reenact, some of the most conservative discursive modes available to American intellectuals. Though the Black American may be cool and cosmopolitan, these attributes are always underwritten not only by (sexual) primitivism but also, I would argue, by a relentlessly consistent perception of the black as nearly voiceless and certainly choiceless victim.

Watching throughout this piece of performance art have been the two white policemen who will in just a few moments falsely arrest Sweetback and thus begin the drama of hide-and-seek that is the substance of this film. They lean heavily on Sweetback's boss, Beetle, to allow them to take the man with them in a cynical attempt to demonstrate their concern for black-on-black violence. Like the rest of Beetle's audience, however, they enjoy the spectacle that Sweetback, the fairy, and the two women put on and comport themselves with Beetle and later with Sweetback in a manner that suggests a sort of honor among thieves—that is, until the show ends and the Good Dyke Fairy Godmother invites members of the audience to come and test Sweetback's prowess. The clumsiness with which Van Peebles then handles what had up until this point been a somewhat clever moment ought to alert us, I believe, to the real ideological work that he attempts to accomplish here. Immediately upon the fairy's offer, a white woman jumps up and begins to disrobe, even as her companion attempts to hold her back. The policemen, seeing this, turn inexplicably hostile, and with a gesture from Beetle, the Good Dyke Fairy Godmother delivers her lines as if she is carefully removing fish bones from her mouth: "But . . . uh . . . That is to say . . . uh. . . . This offer is only open to . . . uh . . . sisters." At which point the crowd breaks into sheets of laughter.

We seem then to have returned to where we began. That menacing policeman has reentered the scene, turning people black willy-nilly with his steely, penetrating gaze. Moreover, he has collected his beloved, Sweetback, and won out again over the too-clumsy solicitations of the dreaded white female interloper. To his credit, Van Peebles does yeoman's work in the process of alerting us to the fact that this struggle between policeman and captive, master and slave, involves a homoerotic ritual that can be remarked, laughed at, even celebrated but never truly relinquished. Indeed part of the way that Van Peebles marks himself as contemporary and hip is precisely the ease with which he announces both the homoerotic and the homosexual, an ease that he will maintain throughout *Sweet Sweetback*.

The difficultly is that in the process of declaiming his own liberalism, Van Peebles finds it necessary to repeat and to celebrate the worn-out notion of the black avenger's noble and innocent struggle with the white policeman. Moreover, he gets away with this altogether clumsy procedure precisely because he frames it within a queer black spectacle that does the work of alerting the audience to how modern and advanced the aesthetic apparatus on display actually is. It only takes one moment of consideration, however, to understand the simplicity of this line of thought. The Los Angeles police officer who freely enters a notorious house of prostitution, catering to an interracial "queer" clientele, and who engages with both its proprietor and its workers in the friendliest of manners but who is shocked beyond belief at the idea of a white woman who might want to have sex with a black man seems a bit of a stretch to me even in early-1970s America. More to the point, the narrative that I have just offered flies in the face of the realities of the interracial community that the cast and the crew of *Sweet Sweetback* formed at least during the movie's filming, not to mention the interracial and transnational community of which Melvin Van Peebles was so famously a part, as evinced most provocatively by his Mexico City–born son, Mario.

One of the more interesting and more telling silences attending the rhetorical strategies that underwrite the supposed originality of *Sweet Sweetback* is the fact that this feature was not Van Peebles's first but instead his third. It was preceded by *The Story of a Three Day Pass* (1968) and the better-known *Watermelon Man* (1970).[7] I should warn my readers that it is possible to be a bit stunned when viewing these films, as I did, in reverse order. Where *Sweet Sweetback* comes decked out in all the fine regalia of blackness and soul, both *Watermelon Man* and especially *The Story of a Three Day Pass* look surprisingly like the integrationist films of the 1950s of which *Sweet Sweetback* is so clearly a critique. In both of these earlier features, the focus is precisely *not* on the matter of black independence, cultural or otherwise, but on how Black Americans might, in fact, be integrated into the mainstreams of American and European society.

Briefly, *The Story of a Three Day Pass* treats of a black soldier stationed in France, who on the verge of a promotion is given a pass to go to Paris by his commanding officer. There he meets an enchanting French girl, and the two begin a brief affair. The work is both tragic and archly comic (a trait that is largely absent in *Sweet Sweetback*), featuring not only a brutally short interracial love affair but also the staging of each of the lovers' fantasies of one another as they take to the bedroom. The young black military man imagines himself a fine gentleman, living proudly on a grand estate, as he lays his head next to the lovely tresses of his beloved. She, meanwhile, sees herself surrounded by half-dressed savages, eager to feast on an unlikely meal of tender white meat. The pretty affair between the two is brought up short, however, when white soldiers from the base see the couple together and report the matter to their commander. The young man is then ordered to remain in his quarters until a group of visiting black churchwomen arrive and persuade the commander to give our hero his liberty. He then runs in a fit of ecstasy to phone his lovely white prize, only to be met by the ugly voice of a man on the other end of the telephone line who has the ignoble responsibility of informing the soldier that the girl has given him the wrong number. In *Watermelon Man,* Van Peebles reverses this joke, offering us a white racist character, played by famed black comedian Godfrey Chambers, who wakes up after a day of too much tanning to find that he has in fact, turned black. He is then met with all the racism, hostility, and stupidity that he had once dispensed, until finally he decides to accept the "truth" of who he is and transitions fully into a hip, urban, soulful black cat.

What I would ask you to consider then is that Sweetback does not, in fact, spend all his energy running from the reality of white violence. Instead I would argue that what Sweetback also runs from, what he also fears, is that equally real, equally palpable reality of the Black American's culpability, his lack of innocence. As this brief sketch of Van Peebles's own filmography is meant to suggest, the difficulty faced by the midcentury Black American intellectual was the recognition that, the power of the erotic being what it is, supposed black and white combatants might indeed have become so intimate by the early 1970s that it was difficult, if not impossible, to see where black innocence began and white guilt ended. Van Peebles gestures toward this fact with the inclusion of two black policemen who one at first assumes will have a substantial role in Sweetback's pursuit if not his apprehension but who, we soon enough find, exist only to represent the undeniable truth that there are Black Americans who are part of the system. There are, if you will, black clerks. This is, I hope, a rather simple point to understand. What I think is a more difficult matter, however, is that by tethering the question of the black's innocence to the presumed fact of his potent sexuality, Van Peebles not only invites his audience to situate *Sweet Sweetback's* aesthetics in the same midcentury moment that produced *The White Negro,* he also demonstrates a certain fretfulness about the ways in which his own discussions and elaborations of sexual liberation were abutted by those of both interracialists and homosexuals.

Thus the trick for Van Peebles, as for a great many of his peers, was again to move without moving. This is, I argue, why queers are so overabundant in not only *Sweet Sweetback* but throughout Van Peebles's oeuvre. Tellingly, the young, naive soldier of *The Story of a Three Day Pass,* uncertain of where to go in supercosmopolitan Paris, ends up in a *pissoir,* exchanging furtive glances with the several men who are obviously there to make sexual contact. Later, homosexuals make another unexpected entry into the static narrative of *Sweet Sweetback,* in the personages of three brightly dressed young men seated at a diner, who when asked if they have seen Sweetback answer, "No child, I mean officer. I haven't seen a Mister Sweetback. If you see him send him here. Won't I do officer?" Again Van Peebles gestures broadly in the direction of the homosexual, allowing his camera to linger for long moments on the heavily made-up faces of these young men, beaming rich and ready under bright lights. The point of course is that the outlaw terrains that Van Peebles examines in both films, the Parisian *pissoir* and the Los Angeles suburbs, were of course inhabited by both homosexuals *and* blacks, making it difficult for the uninformed observer to tell exactly who was who.

I would submit to you, therefore, that Van Peebles rehashes the image of the spectacular homosexual as a means by which to avoid fully avowing the interracialism that is one of the major dangers of a potent black sexuality. I have suggested already that the very fact of *Sweet Sweetback's* production is evidence of a level of interracial cooperation and indeed interracial eroticism that is largely unacknowledged in the film. I have also suggested that by depending as heavily as he does on the stereotype of a potent, primitive black sexuality that Van Peebles forces the crossing of race/sex boundaries, a crossing that in the context of mid-twentieth-century America might rightly and readily be read as queer.

You will recall the rejected advances of the white woman during the performance-art scene. Later, while Sweetback is running with Mumu in tow, he encounters a white motorcycle gang. They challenge him to battle their chief, a particularly ferocious, red-headed woman. When asked how he prefers to fight, with knives or chains, clubs or fists, he answers with one of his few lines, "Fucking." Thus in a strange twist we again find the screen filled with Van Peebles's buttocks, a woman's breasts and legs, and the excited, desperate faces of a crowd of onlookers. In the process, Van Peebles makes clear one of the main points of *Once You Go Black*. The image of master embracing slave is reiterated as often and as forcefully as it is precisely because it speaks just as readily to the matter of interracial longing and sexual desire as it does to the question of economic and social repression. The problem of course is that once one acknowledges the erotic component of this, our most sacred myth of origin, it becomes infinitely more difficult to delineate how, when, why, and where power makes itself known. This then is why after the gang breaks their deal with Sweetback, betraying him and alerting the police to his presence, this red-headed, foul-mouthed criminal, whom Sweetback has bested in the most ancient of American games, proves to be honorable in her own way, sending a black biker, played by John Amos, who transports the injured Mumu to safety. This scene, though strange, would be inconsequential if it were not for the reality that *Sweet Sweetback* was not a simple piece of pornography, as Van Peebles assured his financial backers, but instead a film in which the Black Community and Brer Soul take place of honor. If one allows, however, that one of the work's only heroines is a white woman, then this basic logic is thrown into disarray. Van Peebles, however, clever director that he is, does not worry about explaining away this troubling lapse in the work's logic. Instead he allows it to be eclipsed by the spectacular images of the homosexual, whose passages make the eyes pop, even if the lips do not necessarily smack. "No child, I mean officer. I haven't seen a Mister Sweetback. If you see him, send him here. Won't I do officer?"

I will end with a question. What sort of moment is this in which to pose the question of a queer black studies? It is certainly, as I have said, not a moment to allow ourselves to get trapped within either the cynicism or the apathy that are currently so much a part of the practice of American Studies. It is, however, a moment to be suspicious. For as I have attempted to demonstrate in this chapter, one of the ways in which black and gay people have been allowed to be seen within American popular culture is precisely as sentinels at a doorway that leads directly back to some of our most retrograde notions about country and culture. Thus I would say that if there is to be a Queer Black Studies, and I place my emphasis on the word "if," then it must necessarily be corrosive. It must approach with the greatest of trepidation notions such as innocence, tradition, community, and home. And if we are called upon to carry our small lights into the darkness of American Studies, let us always be mindful that those sparklers, lovely, bright, and festive as they are, do, in fact, burn.

Conclusion

Deviant Desiring

> The law is clearly a system of desire, in which provocation and voyeurism have their own place: the phantasy of the cop is not some creation of the homosexual's deranged mind, but the reality of a deviant desiring on the part of police and judiciary.
>
> —Guy Hocquenghem, *Homosexual Desire*

I invite you to imagine a rather comically American scenario. The intellectual, a promising young man of color, has made his way to one of the great capitals of Europe. He has established himself in a borrowed apartment, learned the rudiments of the native language, surrounded himself with books and music, all American of course, and settled down to write. But he is, as is often the case with Americans caught in that peculiar vertigo caused by travel, distracted. The news from home is not good. The rank stench of war reaches him from every corner. Troops mass on enemy borders; bombs explode on buses, killing housewives and office workers; missiles are fired into camps, dismembering refugees who look disturbingly similar to our intrepid intellectual. A great gray cloud of terrorism answered by terror hangs over his country, over countries he has never seen, and even over the airy, bright apartment that he has borrowed here in the center of this still war-scarred European capital.

He has written during his year abroad (indeed the first he has ever had) a study of Black American intellectuals who came of age after the last of the great wars. He pays homage to that generation of artists and critics to whom he feels most indebted, those who had grappled most assiduously with matters of race, gender, and sexuality, those who had been celebrated in his childhood as fine examples of genius, Black, American, genius. But in his struggles to complete the mundane work of cataloging the efforts of midcentury Black American artists, he has been stunned, provoked he should say, by the sheer depth of political and intellectual pessimism that he has encountered, even and especially here, alone on the wrong side of the Atlantic in an apartment that he has come finally to dislike.

The great wheel of history turns at breakneck speed; horror dressed in finely cut robes of red, white, and blue arrives daily at our doorsteps, but no one seems prepared to pay the bill. On the contrary, it appears that Americans are no longer content simply to dismiss the ugliest aspects of contemporary politics and culture. Our knee-jerk disavowals of choice and responsibility ("Not in my name") have come, I suspect, to sound rather shallow when expressed in relation to the radical geopolitical restructurings currently being led by our own nation. Thus all too often contemporary cultural critics fall prey to the pernicious tendency to project our own generation's fictions of lethargy and powerlessness both backwards and forwards, touching both our ancestors and our progeny. This explains why the Black American, here and there, now and then, with all the polite rhetoric of cultural relativism notwithstanding, continues as an only half-formed subject, one who might be chosen but who strangely enough seems never to choose. Indeed he is a subject whose most basic identity claims have been thrust upon him, making it necessary that his so-called agency remain subsumed within that deviant desiring of the police and the judiciary that Guy Hocquenghem so ably narrates.

Still, our promising young intellectual has not attempted simply to remark well-established traditions of Black American autonomy. He has not concerned himself, as is the case with many students of Black American literature and culture, with demarcating the boundaries of profound black tradition. Instead he has struggled in *Once You Go Black* to meet the racialists, and most particularly the white supremacists, on the very ground that they have demarcated. Picking up on one of the major themes of the previous chapter, he suggests that if it is indeed true that the black, like the homosexual, is established within the policeman's steely gaze, this nonetheless does not rob the black subject of agency and choice. Deviancy does not disrupt ontology. On the contrary, as an entire generation of scholars has demonstrated, within even the most rigid social hierarchies there nonetheless exist those many folds, tears, points of peculiarity and funniness that might be put to the service of both master *and* servant, man *and* woman, white *and* black. Even if we are forced to agree that all of what we in this country euphemistically call "race relations" is a reenactment of the master's first attack on his slave, this does not mean that master and slave might not move a bit, might not attempt to negotiate those all-important, indeed life-enabling, interstitial spaces established by and within the interracial embrace.

The preceding chapters have been designed then not only to demonstrate the rather obvious ways that rivalry and desire structure American culture but also to recognize some of the "queer" narratives that are obscured by our overprivileging of traditional scripts of racialized Oedipal rivalry. Indeed where much within the study of Black American literature and culture has been overdetermined by largely unexamined assumptions of a profound and unchanging hostility between black and white male (erotic) combatants, *Once You Go Black* focuses on the ways that Black American intellectuals have attempted to disrupt these narratives. Thus in *The Long Dream,* Richard Wright frames his treatment of the sensuality and violence of midcentury Mississippi with the ethically ambiguous figures of the homosexual and the expatriate. In his late, unfinished novel, *Juneteenth,* Ralph Ellison edits ancient narratives of paternity and cultural reproduction by presenting us with the white son of a black father, in this way moving his aesthetic away from the traditionalist assumptions suggested by the blues and toward the iconoclasm and awkward sense of possibility that attends cinema. James Baldwin plumbs the depths of the gospel tradition in his last novel, *Just above My Head,* only to reiterate his passionate belief that black tradition is itself dependent upon the encouragement of fierce independence and peculiar intellectualism.

Of course many younger intellectuals of the 1960s and 1970s simply refused to pick up on the many fine clues left by Wright, Ellison, and Baldwin. Instead partisans of the Blacks Arts Movement, among others, struggled to reestablish the profundity of black tradition by returning again and again to the certainty of the black body, the comfort of biologistic racialism, such that many lost sight of the strangeness and awkwardness that necessarily confronts even those black-bodied intellectuals who would announce themselves as somehow representative or typical. As with a host of black writers, artists, and political activists, most especially Huey Newton, the discourse of a transhistorical African corporeality often worked to so discount individuality and peculiarity that it ultimately proved to be toxic to the very leaders and intellectuals it was designed to support. This helps us to understand better why when Melvin Van Peebles pressed these discursive and ideological tendencies to their limits, he ended up creating a character in Sweetback who was a wholly flat, dry, and even dull figure, nothing but soul and tradition contained within the savage, highly sexed African body of old.

And therein lies the key to understanding at least *some* of the odd rhetorical and ethical choices that stud *Once You Go Black*. That is to say, it is here, at that difficult juncture where we are asked to decide between ancient African heroics or the mundane narratives of the Black American's everyday forms of choosing, that our promising young intellectual has established his own critique. Indeed he refuses to privilege the rhetorics of return and nostalgia that so burden much contemporary criticism of Black American literature and culture. He is not nostalgic for an ever-beckoning Africa. He does not mourn fallen martyrs, nor does he tremble in the face of forgetfulness, alienation, isolation, peculiarity, funniness, or estrangement. He also understands all too clearly the manner in which martial narratives of men at combat work to obscure the much more complicated realities of how race, gender, and sexuality are actually enacted in this country. Thus he has tried in *Once You Go Black* to wean his readers from the assumption that the less-than-spectacular tools with which we fashion culture and politics are always lacking because they are neither noble nor profound. Instead he has suggested that the notion that the Black American must forever despise what he holds in his hands in favor of what is always already lost is, in fact, part of the very defeatist nonsense that would not only disallow any true form of Black American intellectualism but that would also disqualify Black Americans as self-conscious agents of history. The politics of *Once You Go Black* might be summed up then with the simple observation that the real action of both politics and culture always takes place at the surface and in the present. Though our efforts at memorialization and recovery may prove to be incredibly important therapeutic strategies, they nonetheless would be hard-pressed to stop a war.

One Last Lie

When I began this work I sat at a borrowed desk in a borrowed apartment in the middle of a still war-scarred European capital. Today I am in my own home, though strangely it seems I am a visitor here as well, and even stranger, the city in which I live seems scarred beyond recognition. Once again a soft gray light flows in through the window, resting uneasily on the small dog and cat, both Americans, with whom I share this space. It all reminds me of winters in North Carolina and the troublesome childhood memory that motivates this study.

She said to us—Mrs. Hall was her name, the name of my favorite teacher, who explained the difference between England, Scotland, and Wales as she dumped peanuts into the thin neck of her Coca-Cola bottle—that today we would all tell where we came from. We looked at her, pink faces beaming, brown ones dour. Mrs. Hall, oblivious to the many tiny hostilities directed at her, continued with her friendly, innocuous ritual. Finally arriving at me, the lone brown face at the table for the gifted, she asked where my people came from. I lied, answering that I did not know. Mrs. Hall, delicate hand placed at nape of graceful neck, responded incredulously, "You too, Robert?!" marveling that even I could not properly reproduce the commonsense narratives of predetermination in which she was instructing us. Strangely enough, when she got to my friend Bobby, the lone pink face at the table for the remedial students, he also lied and answered that he was impossibly Scotch Irish on his daddy's side and French Cherokee on his mama's—impossible because Bobby knew even less than I did about the Scotch, Irish, the French, or the long-since-vanquished Cherokee. Still, Mrs. Hall nodded knowingly, as the room seemed filled to overflowing with this Scotch-Irish-French-Cherokee tribe, and continued examining genealogies while swallowing Coca-Cola-soaked peanuts.

From that day to this, there has not been a single month of my life in which I have not recalled that incident and wondered what would have happened if Bobby and I had told the truth, nothing ugly, nothing grand, just the dumb, simple truth. Two farms backed one against the other, one black, the other white. The white one still supporting a cow or two, the black one long since resigned to raising front-yard chickens and backyard hogs, all fed on scraps left by the brown/red/yellow/black family that lived inside. Perhaps Bobby might have mentioned the arrival of a city cousin, also named Bobby, who in the face of his cousin's taunts—Black Bobby/White Bobby Sittin in a Tree/K-I-S-S-I-N-G—had promptly changed his name to Robert, a change that stuck. Or maybe Robert might have detailed peeing contests (You too, Robert?!) and the long, fascinating arch and range of Bobby's yellow stream. Both might have remembered swinging like Africans on the vines that hung uneasily in the woods behind the two farms, sometimes Tarzan, other times Jane, depending on the one's relative position to the other. But instead they were both caught up in a force (desire, some might call it) that they could not have named, a power so strange and seemingly invincible that they substituted rank lies for the simple truth that they might have offered: "Mrs. Hall, I'm from here."

I return to the farm of my country cousins. They have all moved to the city, leaving behind my ancient brown/red/yellow/black aunts who sit on their porches, taking in the soft gray light of the North Carolina winter. They explain fretfully that all their good neighbors have sold their land to developers and point across the field to the tacky development of instantly produced southern mansions that has encircled the farm. On the road that passes by the small house where we are sitting a Saab slows a bit to better take in the rustic tableau produced by me and my aunts, one of whom—the black one, I believe—spits on cue into a small tin bucket she keeps beside the La-Z-Boy recliner inherited from a long-dead uncle.

Another, perhaps the brown one, says, "We got nothing but rich white folks around here now."

"Lord ain't that the truth," answers the red.

I sit on the steps, taking in the last of the weak light before the chill of night sets in. Then the oldest aunt, the yellow one with the bad temperament, the tobacco-stained teeth, and the long Indian nose, the witch of the family, finishes the conversation by doing what she does best, stating the obvious.

"I miss *my* white folks," she says, referring to Bobby and his family with their dogs, good manners, and Christmastime gifts of quail and sweet-potato pie.

We all sit silently for a while until I, out of rhythm and with an incongruous formality that my family has come to expect, reiterate the similarity between myself and my mean, long-nosed, yellow aunt.

"Yes, ma'am," I mumble. "I know what you mean."

Notes

Notes to the Introduction

1. See Frederick Douglass, *Narrative of the Life of Frederick Douglass, An American Slave, Written by Himself,* ed. William L. Andrews and William S. Mcfeely (1845; reprint, New York: Norton, 1994).

2. See René Girard, *Deceit, Desire and the Novel: Self and Other in Literary Structure,* trans. Yvonne Frecerro (Baltimore: Johns Hopkins University Press, 1965).

3. Slavoj Z̆iz̆ek, *The Ticklish Subject: The Absent Centre of Political Ontology* (New York: Verso, 1999).

4. Ralph Ellison, "Some Questions and Some Answers," in Ralph Ellison, *Shadow and Act* (New York: Vintage, 1972).

5. Thomas Holt, *The Problem of Race in the Twenty-First Century* (Cambridge, MA: Harvard University Press, 2000), 10.

6. See Howard Sitkoff, *A New Deal for Blacks: The Emergence of Civil Rights as a National Issue* (New York: Oxford University Press, 1978); Gerald Jaynes and Robin M. Williams, eds., *A Common Destiny: Blacks and American Society* (Washington, DC: National Academy Press, 1989).

7. See Manning Marable, *How Capitalism Underdeveloped Black America: Problems in Race, Political Economy and Society* (Boston: South End Press, 1983).

8. See Robert F. Reid-Pharr, *Conjugal Union: The Body, the House and the Black American* (New York: Oxford University Press, 1999).

9. Tellingly, Homer Plessy's case was supported by the Creole-dominated Comite des Citoyens of New Orleans that had been founded in 1890 to fight for both the political and economic advancement of "people of color" in Louisiana. See Arnold R. Hirsh and Joseph Logsdon, eds., *Creole New Orleans: Race and Americanization* (Baton Rouge: Louisiana State University Press, 1992).

10. See Robert F. Reid-Pharr, "Cosmopolitan, Afrocentric Mulatto Intellectual," in Robert F. Reid-Pharr, *Black Gay Man: Essays* (New York: New York University Press, 2001), 44–61.

11. See Wilson Jeremiah Moses, *Afrotopia: The Roots of African American Popular History* (New York: Oxford University Press, 1998).

12. See especially Marable, *How Capitalism Underdeveloped Black America*; Robert L. Allen, *Black Awakening in Capitalist America: An Analytic History* (Trenton, NJ: Africa World Press, 1990); George Jackson, *Soledad Brother: The Prison Letters of George Jackson* (1970; reprint, Chicago: Lawrence Hill Books, 1994).

13. Quoted in Allen, *Black Awakening,* 102.

14. Quoted in ibid., 103. For more on the relationship of Black Americans to the Communist Party, see Harold Cruse, *The Crisis of the Negro Intellectual: A Historical Analysis of the Failure of Black Leadership* (New York: Quill, 1984); Robin D. G. Kelley, *Alabama Communists during the Great Depression* (Chapel Hill: University of North Carolina Press, 1990); Mark Naison, *Communists in Harlem during the Depression* (Urbana: University of Illinois Press, 1983).

15. Harold Cruse, *The Crisis of the Negro Intellectual* (New York: Morrow, 1967).

16. Booker T. Washington, *Up from Slavery* (1901; reprint, New York: Penguin, 1986).

17. John A. Williams, *The Man Who Cried I Am* (New York: Thunder's Mouth Press, 1967). Hereafter cited in text.

18. The character of Margrit obviously references Richard Wright's friend and translator Margrit Sabloniere, whom Wright met in Holland and who was purported to be among Wright's closest friends when he died in 1960. See Hazel Rowley, *Richard Wright: The Life and Times* (New York: Henry Holt, 2001), 510–513.

19. See Eve Kosofsky Sedgwick, *Between Men: English Literature and Male Homosocial Desire* (New York: Columbia University Press, 1985); and Eve Kosofsky Sedgwick, *Epistemology of the Closet* (Berkeley: University of California Press, 1990).

20. See James Sallis, *Chester Himes: A Life* (New York: Walker, 2000). The character also builds upon the figure of Leroy Haynes, a Black American GI who, Michel Fabre tells us, stayed in Paris after the war and with his French wife opened a restaurant that became an important meeting place for Black American expatriates. Strangely Fabre misses the well-known fact that Haynes's doppelganger, Gordon Heath, an actor and singer who opened an important "soul" café in Paris, did so with his male lover. See Michel Fabre, *Black American Writers in France: 1840–1980* (Chicago: University of Illinois Press, 1991), 165, 167.

Notes to Chapter 1

1. I am trying to follow some of the clues left by Kenneth Warren, who writes of the emphasis on cultural politics within Black American intellectual life, "Scholars have been inclined to treat any recurrence as evidence that the truth about black political hopes and desires lies hidden within apparently nonpolitical activities. *These studies though historical in intent, tend to freeze and generalize specific moments in the historical experience of Black people, and then to read the whole of that history through the lens of this crystallization.*" See Kenneth Warren, *So Black and Blue: Ralph Ellison and the Occasion of Criticism* (Chicago: University of Chicago Press, 2003), 33; emphasis mine.

2. Margaret Walker, *Richard Wright, Daemonic Genius: A Portrait of the Man and a Critical Look at His Work* (New York: Amistad, 1988).

3. Jean-Paul Sartre, *Literature and Existentialism,* trans. Bernard Frechtman (New York: Citadel, 1977), 77.

4. Saunders Redding, review of *The Long Dream,* in Henry Louis Gates and K. A. Appiah, eds., *Richard Wright: Critical Perspectives Past and Present* (New York: Amistad, 1993), 61.

5. Richard Wright, "The Literature of the Negro in the United States," in Richard Wright, *White Man Listen! Lectures in Europe, 1950–1956* (New York: Harper, 1957), 74.

6. Quoted in Walker, *Richard Wright,* 144.

7. The story that Walker tells is that she arrived in New York from Chicago to attend one of the most important writers' gatherings of the twentieth century and to see again her dear friend and colleague Dick Wright. A variety of mundane misunderstandings and coincidences, all of which Walker is careful to narrate from the vantage point of the naif, lead to Walker's walking unexpectedly into the room of Ted Ward at the Douglas Hotel, where presumably she interrupted a poorly timed tryst between Ward and Wright. Walker, *Richard Wright,* 132.

8. Quoted in Hazel Rowley, *Richard Wright: The Life and Times* (New York: Henry Holt, 2001), 126.

9. Ibid.

10. Richard Wright, *The Long Dream* (Chatham, NJ: Chatham Bookseller, 1969). Hereafter cited in text.

11. George Eliot, review of *Dred: A Tale of the Dismal Swamp,* in Elizabeth Ammons, ed., *Critical Essays on Harriet Beecher Stowe* (Boston: G. K. Hall, 1980), 43.

12. The line that Spillers focuses on is Little Eva's entreaty to her father, St. Clare, upon seeing Tom, "You have money enough, I know. I want him." Quoted in Hortense Spillers, "Changing the Letter: The Yokes, the Jokes of Discourse, or, Mrs. Stow, Mr. Reed," in Hortense Spillers, *Black, White, and in Color: Essays on American Literature and Culture* (Chicago: University of Chicago Press, 2003), 191.

13. Sherley Anne Williams, "Papa Dick and Sister-Woman: Reflections on Women in the Fiction of Richard Wright," in Arnold Rampersad, ed., *Richard Wright: A Collection of Critical Essays* (Englewood Cliffs, NJ: Prentice Hall, 1995), 65–66.

14. Hortense Spillers, "Mama's Baby, Papa's Maybe: An American Grammar Book," in Hortense Spillers, *Black, White, and in Color: Essays on American Literature and Culture* (Chicago: University of Chicago Press, 2003), 228.

15. The phrase is Michael Warner's. See Michael Warner, ed., *Fear of a Queer Planet: Queer Politics and Social Theory* (Minneapolis: University of Minnesota Press, 1993).

Notes to Chapter 2

1. Lawrence Jackson, *Ralph Ellison: Emergence of Genius* (New York: Wiley, 2002).

2. Jerry Gafio Watts, *Heroism and the Black Intellectual: Ralph Ellison, Politics, and Afro-American Intellectual Life* (Chapel Hill: University of North Carolina Press, 1994).

3. Ralph Ellison, *Juneteenth: A Novel* (New York: Vintage, 1999). Hereafter cited in text.

4. Albert Murray, *The Omni-Americans: Black Experience and American Culture* (1970; reprint, New York: Da Capo, 1990), 148, 152.

5. Ibid., 166–167.

6. Ralph Ellison, *Shadow and Act* (New York: Vintage, 1972), xx.

7. Carla Capetti, "Sociology of Existence: Wright and the Chicago School of Sociology," in Henry Louis Gates and K. A. Appiah, eds., *Richard Wright: Critical Perspectives* (New York: Amistad, 1993), 255–271.

8. Ralph Ellison, *Going to the Territory* (New York: Random House, 1986), 304.

9. James Baldwin, "Everybody's Protest Novel," in James Baldwin, *Notes of a Native Son* (Boston: Beacon, 1955), 22.

10. Quoted in Jackson, *Ralph Ellison,* 143.

11. Ellison, *Shadow and Act,* 94.

12. Ibid., 16.

13. I am referencing the fact that it was Hemingway who first made the suggestion that the relationship between Huck and Jim stands at the center of all serious American literary practice. See Ernest Hemingway, *The Green Hills of Africa* (New York: Scribner, 1935).

14. Leslie Fiedler, "Come Back to the Raft Ag'in, Huck Honey!" *Partisan Review* 15 (June 1948): 664–671.

15. See Eve Kosofsky Sedgwick, *Between Men: English Literature and Male Homosocial Desire* (New York: Columbia University Press, 1985); and Eve Kosofsky Sedgwick, *Epistemology of the Closet* (Berkeley: University of California Press, 1990).

16. Ellison, *Shadow and Act,* 100.

17. Ellison, *Going to the Territory,* 93–94.

18. Watts, *Heroism and the Black Intellectual,* 107.

Notes to Chapter 3

1. See Paul Gilroy, *The Black Atlantic: Modernity and Double Consciousness* (Cambridge, MA: Harvard University Press, 1993).

2. See Paul Gilroy, *Against Race: Imagining Political Culture beyond the Color Line* (Cambridge, MA: Harvard University Press, 2000).

3. James Baldwin, *Just above My Head* (New York: Dial, 1979). Hereafter cited in text.

4. See Michael G. Cooke, *Afro-American Literature in the Twentieth Century: The Achievement of Intimacy* (New Haven, CT: Yale University Press, 1984).

5. See Judith Butler, *Bodies That Matter: On the Discursive Limits of "Sex"* (New York: Routledge, 1993); Elaine Scarry, *The Body in Pain: The Making and Unmaking of the World* (New York: Oxford University Press, 1985); Peter Brooks, *Body Work: Objects of Desire in Modern Narrative* (Cambridge, MA: Harvard University Press, 1993).

6. Quoted in James Campbell, *Talking at the Gates: A Life of James Baldwin* (New York: Viking, 1991), 202.

7. See Emily Brontë, *Wuthering Heights* (1847; reprint, New York: Penguin, 1995).

Notes to Chapter 4

1. Charles Johnson, *Being and Race: Black Writing Since 1970* (Bloomington: Indiana University Press, 1990), 5.

2. Stuart Hall, "What Is This 'Black' in Black Popular Culture?" in Valerie Smith, ed., *Representing Blackness: Issues in Film and Video* (New Brunswick, NJ: Rutgers University Press, 1997).

3. Frantz Fanon, *The Wretched of the Earth* (New York: Grove, 1963), 49–50.

4. See Frantz Fanon, *Black Skin/White Masks,* trans. C. L. Markmann (New York: Grove, 1967).

5. George Jackson, *Soledad Brother: The Prison Letters of George Jackson* (1970; reprint, Chicago: Lawrence Hill Books, 1994), 223–224.

6. Judith Butler, *Excitable Speech: A Politics of the Performative* (New York: Routledge, 1997), 11.

7. Calvin C. Hernton, *Sex and Racism in America* (New York: Anchor, 1965), 39.

8. See Wilson Jeremiah Moses, *Afrotopia: the Roots of African American Popular History* (New York: Cambridge University Press, 1998), 214.

9. Norman Mailer, *The White Negro* (San Francisco: City Lights Books, 1957).

10. Michelle Wallace, *Black Macho and the Myth of the Superwoman* (New York: Dial, 1979).

11. Excerpt from Nikki Giovanni, "The True Import of Present Dialogue, Black vs. Negro (For Peppe, Who Will Ultimately Judge Our Efforts)," in Nikki Giovanni, *Black Feeling, Black Talk, Black Judgement: Poems* (New York: Morrow, 1979), 19–20.

12. Jane Gallop, *The Daughter's Seduction: Feminism and Psychoanalysis* (Ithaca, NY: Cornell University Press, 1982), 38.

13. Fanon, *Black Skin/White Masks,* 116.

14. Elaine Brown, *A Taste of Power: A Black Woman's Story* (New York: Pantheon, 1992), 398.

15. Giovanni, "Seduction," in *Black Feeling,* 38.

16. See Imamu Amiri Baraka, *The Autobiography of LeRoi Jones/Amiri Baraka* (Chicago: Lawrence Hill Books, 1997); Wallace, *Black Macho;* Audre Lorde, *Zami: A New Spelling of My Name* (Watertown, MA: Persephone, 1982); James Baldwin, *Notes of a Native Son* (1955; reprint, Boston: Beacon, 1984); Malcolm X, *The Autobiography of Malcolm X* (New York: Ballantine, 1965); Eldridge Cleaver, *Soul on Ice* (New York: McGraw-Hill, 1967); Brown, *A Taste of Power.*

17. My thinking here owes much to Siobhan Somerville's wonderful thesis in *Queering the Color Line* that there is no essential disconnect within the American imagination or within the law around matters of race and sexuality. See Siobhan Somerville, *Queer-*

ing the Color Line: Race and the Making of Homosexuality in America (Durham, NC: Duke University Press, 1999).

18. Giovanni, "Of Liberation," in *Black Feeling,* 45.

19. Giovanni, "Woman Poem," in *Black Feeling,* 78.

20. Huey P. Newton, "The Women's Liberation and Gay Liberation Movements," in Huey P. Newton, *To Die for the People: The Writings of Huey P. Newton* (New York: Random House, 1972).

21. For a good example of work that attempts to resuscitate a positive image of contemporary Black American nationalism, see William L. Van Deburg, *New Day in Babylon: The Black Power Movement and American Culture, 1965–1975* (Chicago: University of Chicago Press, 1992). For a work that particularly stresses the human weaknesses of Huey Newton and rehearses again the fact of his criminality, see Hugh Pearson, *The Shadow of the Panther: Huey Newton and the Price of Black Power in America* (New York: Addison-Wesley, 1994).

22. See Huey P. Newton, *Revolutionary Suicide* (New York: Harcourt Brace Jovanovich, 1973); Huey P. Newton, *To Die for the People: The Writings of Huey P. Newton* (New York: Random House, 1972).

Notes to Chapter 5

1. See Louis Althusser, "Ideology and Ideological State Apparatuses," in Louis Althusser, *Lenin and Philosophy and Other Essays* (New York: Monthly Review Press, 1971).

2. Stuart Hall, "What Is This 'Black' in Black Popular Culture?" in David Morley and Kuan-Hsing Chen, eds., *Stuart Hall: Critical Dialogues in Cultural Studies* (New York: Routledge, 1996), 468.

3. Ibid., 470.

4. Van Peebles takes the matter to the next step in his short "The Real Deal: The Way It Is," in which he informs us not only that the sexual acts in the film were real and not simulated but also that he was infected with a sexually transmitted disease during the filming.

5. See Norman Mailer, *The White Negro* (San Francisco: City Lights Books, 1957).

6. Hall, "What Is This 'Black' in Black Popular Culture?" 471.

7. These features were preceded by three shorts: *Three Pickup Men for Herrick* (1957), *Sunlight* (1957), and *Cinq Cent Balles* (1963).

Index

ABOUT THE AUTHOR

Robert Reid-Pharr is Professor of English and American Studies at the CUNY Graduate Center. He is the author of *Black Gay Man: Essays* (available from NYU Press) and *Conjugal Union: The Body, the House and the Black American.*